TWAYNE'S WORLD AUTHORS SERIES
A Survey of the World's Literature

FRANCE

Maxwell A. Smith, Guerry Professor of French, Emeritus
The University of Chattanooga
Former Visiting Professor in Modern Languages
The Florida State University

EDITOR

Simone de Beauvoir

TWAS 532

SIMONE DE BEAUVOIR

KONRAD BIEBER

State University of New York at Stony Brook

TWAYNE PUBLISHERS
A DIVISION OF G. K. HALL & CO., BOSTON

Published in 1979 by Twayne Publishers,
A Division of G. K. Hall & Co.
All Rights Reserved

Printed on permanent/durable acid-free paper and bound
in the United States of America

First Printing

Frontispiece sketch of Simone
de Beauvoir courtesy of French cultural services.

Library of Congress Cataloging in Publication Data

Bieber, Konrad.
Simone de Beauvoir.

(Twayne's world authors series ; TWAS 532 : France)
Bibliography: p. 191–94
Includes index.
1. Beauvoir, Simone de, 1908–
—Criticism and interpretation. I. Title.
PQ2603.E362Z58   848′.9′1409   78-27470
ISBN 0-8057-6374-0

To my mother

Contents

About the Author

Konrad Bieber is Professor of French and Comparative Literature at the State University of New York at Stony Brook since 1968. He holds a Licence de Lettres from the University of Paris and a Ph.D. degree from Yale University, where he taught for five years. He also taught for four sessions at the Middlebury College French Summer School and for fifteen years at Connecticut College. He contributed a number of articles to journals such as *Revue de Littérature Comparée*, *The French Review*, *Esprit*, and *Comparative Literature Studies*. An earlier book, *L'Allemagne vue par les Ecrivains de la Résistance Française*, appeared in Geneva with a preface by Albert Camus. In 1970, he was made Chevalier des Palmes Académiques.

Preface

Few writers have generated such a division of public opinion over their work as Simone de Beauvoir. For some readers, especially of *Le Deuxième Sexe (The Second Sex)*, she is the champion of the downtrodden, the herald of a new era, a great and good writer, and a "beautiful person." For others, mostly people with conservative ideas but also a few genuine radicals, she represents all that is loathsome, crude, unladylike—the incarnation of evil. Few can remain indifferent to her.

There are ample reasons for such a disparity in the public reception of her work, chiefly the fact of life that the vast majority of both admirers and detractors never read a single line of her books and based their judgment on hearsay,[1] on popular magazine articles, or on plain gossip. One should not blame people for having opinions that are not based on direct knowledge, for influences are felt strongly even by those who never studied the works of thinkers whose doctrines affected them one way or another, as in the case of Nietzsche and his French disciples: the seminal thought was "in the air," as indeed imponderables operate with great effect, positively or negatively.

While Simone de Beauvoir never directly attacks the male world as such, she has, with ever-increasing alacrity and vigor, hammered away at the urgency she sees in establishing completely equal rights for women. Her polemic pursuits are far more all-encompassing, however. She is also the courageous mouthpiece for many causes: she speaks for miners struggling for improvements in coal mines; for workers, men and women alike, who are faced with fire hazards and insalubrious conditions in factories and lofts; for ethnic minorities hounded by French bureaucracy; against war crimes; and last but not least by far, for justice and humane treatment for Israeli war prisoners in Syria, among other expressions of concern regarding the survival of Israel.

No starry-eyed dreamer, Simone de Beauvoir accepts challenges as they arise, never afraid of leading an unpopular fight. Sometimes, her efforts may appear naive and close to ludicrous—witness her and Sartre's acting as barkers for avant-garde papers, provoking confrontation with the police and inviting arrest. Both Sartre and she have been accused, in recent years, of seeking publicity, indeed martyr status.

Simone de Beauvoir has sometimes been described as a mere appendage to Sartre. Jean-Paul Sartre's share in her life is essential. His influence on some of her ideas and works is undeniable, and Simone de Beauvoir would be the last one to deny it. However, she is an entirely independent thinker and an original writer, beholden to no one, whatever one may think of her work.

Her stature rests on the impact she has had on society both by her pen and her voice, raised in defense of victims of prejudice and injustice. As she has published books with varying success since 1943, it is not too early to attempt an appraisal of her work, which, with few exceptions, stands as an integral part of contemporary French literature. At the same time, much of her expressed thought remains tentative, subject to alteration, as she admitted in her *Memoirs*: she is sticking to her guns on essentials while marking changes in her perception as they occur.

The present study of Simone de Beauvoir is bent on careful evaluation of what makes this writer distinct from others. Some of the views expressed here will appear subjective, and no doubt one cannot remain impassive when confronted with ideas as sharply delineated as Simone de Beauvoir's on basic human questions. There will also be discussion of the findings of some of the many critics of her work, whose discoveries have immeasurably helped shape this study.

Substantial reliance on translations of Simon de Beauvoir's work proved inevitable. Most of these translations were done not only competently but also by translators congenial with the author. Whatever small divergencies may have been noted cannot detract from the total merit of the translations.

I owe a great debt to some of the excellent studies on Simone de Beauvoir and am glad to acknowledge this debt here, as I shall also indicate in the body of the study and in the bibliography.

The bulk of the manuscript was read by Professors Eléonore M. Zimmermann and Sverre Lyngstad, who made invaluable suggestions that go a long way to improve the text. I cannot thank them enough for their firm and thoughtful advice and careful, critical reading. Without this very considerable help, this would be a lesser book. All shortcomings are, of course, my responsibility.

Preface

I also would like to take this opportunity to express my deepfelt appreciation to Professor Maxwell A. Smith, editor of the French series of Twayne's World Authors. His understanding, patience, and forbearance are matched only by the diligence of his reading and his constructive criticism. I owe him a very real debt of gratitude for making this book a reality.

KONRAD BIEBER

Stony Brook, New York

Acknowledgments

Simone de Beauvoir, *Memoirs of a Dutiful Daughter* (New York: Harper & Row, 1974). Copyright © 1958 by Librairie Gallimard. Translation © 1959 by The World Publishing Company. Reprinted by permission of Harper & Row, Publishers, Inc.

Simone de Beauvoir, *Force of Circumstance* (New York: Harper & Row, 1977). Copyright © 1963 by Librairie Gallimard. English translation copyright © 1964, 1965 by G. P. Putnam's Sons. Reprinted by permission of Harper & Row, Publishers, Inc.

Simone de Beauvoir, *The Prime of Life* (New York: Harper & Row, 1976). Copyright © 1960 by Librairie Gallimard. English translation copyright © 1962 by The World Publishing Company. Reprinted by permission of Harper & Row, Publishers, Inc.

L'Existentialisme et la Sagesse des Nations (original edition: Paris: Nagel, 1948) Copyright by Librairie Gallimard.

The Second Sex (New York: Alfred A. Knopf, 1953) Copyright 1963 by Alfred A. Knopf.

The Coming of Age (New York: Putnam, 1972) Copyright by Putnam's 1972

(NOTE: By a letter to the Author, dated October 6, 1978, Madame Simone de Beauvoir authorized quotations from the translations of her works.)

Chronology

1905 June 21: Jean-Paul Sartre born in Paris.
1908 January 9: Simone de Beauvoir born in Paris.
1914 Simone enters the Cours Désir.
1918 "Zaza" (Elisabeth Mabille) meets Simone; their friendship starts and lasts until Zaza's death in 1929.
1925 Simone enters the Institut Sainte-Marie in Neuilly, directed by Madame Daniélou. She also attends the Institut Catholique, in Paris, and the Sorbonne.
1929 June: Simone meets Jean-Paul Sartre. Both Sartre and Simone succeed at the *Agrégation de Philosophie* (Sartre had failed at his first try, a year earlier). Death of Zaza. Fall: Simone becomes an assistant at the Lycée Victor Duruy in Paris; she moves into her grandmother's apartment. Sartre and Simone start their relationship—the "two year lease" which lasts to the present. Sartre commences his military service (completed in January 1931) at the meteorological station near Tours.
1931 Summer: first trip to Spain, with Sartre. Sartre begins teaching at the *Lycée* in Le Havre (until 1933); Simone begins teaching at the *Lycée* in Marseille (until 1932).
1932 Summer: trip to the Baleares and to Spanish Morocco, with Sartre; trip with Sartre, Madame Lemaire*, and Pagniez, through Spain. Simone commences teaching at the *Lycée* in Rouen (until 1936).
1933 Easter: trip to London, with Sartre. Summer: trip to Italy, with Sartre. Sartre spends the year at the French Institute in Berlin.
1934 February: Simone (on "sick" leave) visits Berlin; Summer: trip to Germany and Austria, with Sartre. Sartre returns to teach in Le Havre (through 1936).
1935 Easter: trip to the Italian Lakes, with Sartre.
1936 Summer: trip to Rome, Naples, Sicily, with Sartre. Fall: Simone starts teaching at the *Lycée Molière,* in Paris; Sartre teaches at the *Lycée* in Laon.
1937 February-March: Simone has pneumonia. Summer: trip to

Greece, with Sartre and Jacques Bost. Sartre teaches at the *Lycée Pasteur*, in Paris.

1938 Publication of Sartre's *La Nausée*. Summer: trip to French Morocco, with Sartre.

1939 August-September: Sartre is mobilized; he serves in different places, mostly in Lorraine; when Simone visits him, he is at Brumath. Fall: Simone teaches at the *Lycée Camille Sée*, in Paris.

1940 June: like millions of Frenchmen, Simone leaves the city and flees before the German invasion. June 21: Sartre is taken prisoner of war at Padoux, Lorraine. July: after returning from exodus, Simone is appointed at the *Lycée Victor Duruy*, in Paris.

1941 April 1: Sartre is "liberated"; he returns from captivity. July: death of Georges de Beauvoir, Simone's father.

1942 Sartre teaches the "khâgne" class at the *Lycée Condorcet* in Paris (through 1944).

1943 Sartre is also appointed at the *Lycée Pasteur*. Publication of *L'Invitée*.

1944 Simone is suspended from teaching for "corrupting a minor." She works for the national radio network as a features producer. September: Simone is reinstated, but resigns from teaching. Publication of *Pyrrhus et Cinéas*.

1945 February-March: trip to Portugal, via Spain. August: trip to Belgium, with Sartre. September: publication of *Le Sang des Autres*. late Fall: Première of *Les Bouches Inutiles;* Publication of *Les Bouches Inutiles*.

1946 January: lecture tour in Tunisia; May: lecture tour in Switzerland, with Sartre; June: lecture tour in Italy, with Sartre; November; lecture tour in Holland, with Sartre. Publication of *Tous les Hommes sont mortels*.

1947 February-May: first trip to the United States; first encounter with Nelson Algren. Summer: four days in London; August: trip to Denmark, Sweden, Norway. September: second trip to the United States, to see Algren. Publication of *Pour une Morale de l'Ambiguité*.

1948 February: Berlin. Publication of *L'Amérique au Jour le Jour*. Summer: trip with Algren through the U.S. (on the Mississippi), Mexico, and Guatemala. Publication of *L'Existentialisme et la Sagesse des Nations*. Trip to Algeria with Sartre.

Chronology

1949 June: Algren comes to Paris, trip to Italy and North Africa, with Algren. Fall: publication of *Le Deuxième Sexe*.

1950 Spring: African tour, with Sartre: Algiers—Gardhaïa—Gao, Tamanrasset—Bamako—Dakar. Summer: trip to the U.S.; stay in Michigan. "Break" with Algren.

1951 Trip to Norway, Iceland, Scotland, and England. Simone buys her first automobile.

1952 Breast operation (biopsy). Break between Sartre and Camus. Trips by car to Provence and Italy. Fall: start of her relationship with Claude Lanzmann.

1953 June: car tour with Lanzmann to Geneva, Italy, Yugoslavia. Summer: trip to Holland, with Sartre.

1954 January: car tour in Algeria, with Lanzmann; car tour in Spain, with Lanzmann. August: by car with Sartre to Alsace, Germany, Austria, and Czechoslovakia. Fall: Publication of *Les Mandarins*. *Les Mandarins* is awarded the *Prix Goncourt*.

1955 Trip to Helsinki, with Sartre, to attend the Congress of the International Peace Movement. Publication of *Privilèges*.

1956 Summer: trip to Spain, with Lanzmann; trip to China, via the USSR, with Sartre.

1956 Trip to Italy, Yugoslavia, Greece, with Sartre, Lanzmann, and Michèle (ex-Vian).

1957 Trip to Southern Italy and Sicily, with Lanzmann. Summer: in Rome, with Sartre. Publication of *La Longue Marche*.

1958 Publication of *Mémoires d'Une Jeune Fille Rangée*. June: Milan. November: end of relationship with Lanzmann.

1959 Summer: in Rome, with Sartre.

1960 February-March: trip to Cuba, with Sartre. Summer: Simone is visited by Algren in Paris. Trip to Spain with Algren; trip to Greece and Turkey with Algren. Publication (in London) of *Brigitte Bardot and the Lolita Syndrome*. August-September: trip to Brazil, with Sartre; return via Cuba and Spain. Publication of *La Force de l'Age*.

1962 June: trip to the USSR, with Sartre. Summer: in Rome, with Sartre; return with Lanzmann via Italy and Switzerland. Trip to Belgium. Publication of *Djamila Boupacha*, in collaboration with Gisèle Halimi.

1963 Trip to Czechoslovakia with Sartre, death of Françoise de Beauvoir, Simone's mother. Publication of *La Force des Choses*.

1964 Trip to Italy. Trip with Sartre to the USSR, including Estonia. Fall: Sartre refuses the Nobel Prize for Literature. Publication of *Une Mort Très Douce*.

1965 Trip to Northern Italy, with Sartre; on the return trip, alone in her car, Simone has a serious accident, near Chalon sur-Saône. Summer—and practically every summer for some years (to use up Sartre's royalties)—trip to the USSR, this time including Lithuania.

1966 Publication of *Les Belles Images*. Fall: Trip to Japan, with Sartre.

1967 February-March: trip with Sartre to Egypt and Israel. Fall: publication of *La Femme Rcmpue*.

1968 Trip to Yugoslavia.

1969 Summer—as practically every summer, for years—in Rome, with Sartre.

1970 Publication of *La Vieillesse*.

1972 Publication of *Tout Compte Fait*.

1977 A film on Sartre, made by Alexandre Astruc and Michel Contat, with the cooperation of Simone de Beauvoir. (Also appeared in book form, Librairie Gallimard, 1977)

1978 June. A film made by Marianne Ahrne and Pépo Angel, for the photography, and Simone de Beauvoir, for the commentary, *Promenade au Pays de la Vieillesse* is shown in Paris. It is an illustration of some of the highlights in *The Coming of Age*.

1979 A sequel to *The Second Sex* is to be published by Beauvoir.

*Names used by Simone de Beauvoir in her memoirs are used throughout the present study, rather than actual names. Such names are indicated by asterisks throughout.

CHAPTER 1

The First Volume of Memoirs—
Early Life

THE handicap for any man writing about a woman writer is very real. But then, isn't every critic handicapped in some way, being different from his subject socially, psychologically, politically, or philosophically? Whatever qualms the male critic might have, Simone de Beauvoir puts his mind at rest: she speaks and writes in such a way that one might forget about the sex of the novelist or the essayist were it not for the constant concern she voices for the cause of women.

Simone de Beauvoir the novelist uses mostly conventional means of style and setting to convey her message. But the message is unconventional, as are her trailblazing essays on women's condition (*Le Deuxième Sexe* [*The Second Sex*]) and on old age (*La Vieillesse* [*The Coming of Age*]). Her career is best followed through a close study of her memoirs, showing her evolution from a sheltered, coy Catholic to a detached, robust, socially and politically aware agnostic.

The autobiographical writings are probably her finest achievement, together with the two or three novels that are outstanding and the two influential essays mentioned. Few, if any, human beings are known to us as genuinely and as fully as she is through her unabashed notations of a past remembered so vividly, so colorfully, so truly. Some of her more sympathetic critics have compared her to Montaigne, and in fact there is a strong kinship between her and the sixteenth century philosopher. Even the fact that Simone de Beauvoir asked for the advice of her friends before publishing her memoirs does not take away from the disarming candor with which she goes about the task of recording her past. Her concern was to give a truthful account of a life that could, and should, help others

understand much of the twentieth century. Thus, to illustrate the
formation of her mind, no better way can be found than to lean on
her own description of her childhood and adolescence. Her adult
memoirs will serve, along with her whole published work, for an
assessment of her stature as a thinker.

The year 1908, when Simone de Beauvoir was born, belongs to
the *Belle Epoque*. Those were relatively carefree, affluent years
when middle class society lived in an atmosphere of bliss.
Technological and cultural progress is evidenced by the several
world fairs, by the construction of the Eiffel tower as a symbol of the
supremacy of Paris, and by l'art nouveau and its stucco ornaments.
Few Frenchmen remained unbearded; women wore skirts dipping
below their ankles and wide hats over their long hair. This was an
era of stability, of respectability, of financial and economic soundness such as the twentieth century was not to see again.

True, there had been the 1870 defeat and its sequel of social and
political troubles: the Paris Commune; the Panama Scandal, and the
Dreyfus Affair—warnings that all was not well in the best of all
possible orders. And there were distant rumblings from discon-
tented workers who had only just begun to organize into unions. But
basically, the time was one of complacency and building boom. At
any rate the middle classes saw no reason to utter more than perfunctory complaints, such as we may read about in Maupassant's
stories or Courteline's comedies. In fact, the French theatre did not
reveal any deep general or social problems, even though Ibsen's
impact was felt at just about that time. There did not appear, on the
surface at least, any signs of a coming storm.

The First World War brought in its wake fundamental changes in
the socioeconomic structure of French life. The most cruel direct
consequence of the war was to be the loss of so many young men; for
women all over the world this meant involuntary celibacy, since a
whole generation of eligible bachelors had been depleted. Another
effect of the war was that thousands of middle class families were
ruined when their lifetime savings were made worthless through the
Russian Revolution and the subsequent depreciation of Russian
loans and other shares, heretofore considered the safest of invest-
ments. It may be said that more than money was lost; the whole
system of trust in the established order suffered irreparable damage.

While the moral fiber of the prewar period had not been declared void in general, it had sustained irreversible changes. Moral and social habits undreamed of before 1914 became tolerated in Paris. That is not to say that there was any widespread relaxation of moral standards in the average French family. On the contrary, parents continued to exercise the strictest supervision of their children, particularly girls. Not until well after the Second World War can one find any indications of a general breakdown in accepted standards.

To be sure, before 1914 one could find artists, some writers, and a certain number of other nonconformists who lived in defiance of bourgeois morality. But these cases, even though quite numerous in the capital, were virtually nonexistent in the provinces, and they never affected the solid front of public life or of education. The average French bourgeois could spend his whole life without ever coming into contact with any "bohemians." Family relations were a stereotype of authority—the father's—of togetherness, of conventionality.

I *Family Origins*

Simone de Beauvoir's father came from a moderately well to do family. Her great-grandfather had been an inspector of taxes in Argenton in the Creuse department, not far from Limoges. He left his sons "a fairly substantial fortune."[1] Indeed, the younger one was able to live on his income. The older son, Simone's grandfather, inherited among other properties a five hundred acre farm. He married an upper middle class girl from a large family in northern France and became an official in the Paris municipal administration, where he followed a long career crowned by his promotion to department head.

Georges de Beauvoir, Simone's father, was the favorite of his mother and of his teachers. Loathing physical exercise, he was fond of reading and of studying. His mother came from an austere family of devout believers in God and in the virtue of work. Georges every year won prizes at the College Stanislas, the Catholic boys' high school in Paris. During the summer vacations, he taught farm children. He lost his mother when he was thirteen. His father was "half-way between the aristocracy and the bourgeoisie, between the landed gentry and the civil servant. Respecting but not practicing the Catholic religion, he felt himself neither completely integrated with society, nor burdened with any serious responsibilities: he lived a life of epicurean good taste" (35). He was never close to his son. After his mother's death, Georges won no more prizes at school: he no longer felt pushed to do so. Eventually, he studied law and became an attorney (not a shoe manufacturer, as some biographers would have it). But he always dreamed of a stage career. He later confessed to his daughter that if circumstances had permitted it, he would have entered the conservatory. When he felt well established in his position in a law firm, he began taking drama and elocution lessons and playing lead parts in an amateur troop.

In analyzing her father's "strange" vocation, Simone de Beauvoir traces his conflicting ambitions to his social status. By his name, family relations, and certain youthful associations, he was convinced he belonged to the aristocracy. But he soon discovered that he was wanting in some of the essential canons of nobility. His daughter writes:

he adopted their manner of living [the aristocracy's]. He appreciated elegant gestures, charming compliments, social graces, style, frivolity, irony, all the free and easy self-assurance of the rich and the wellborn. The more serious virtues esteemed by the bourgeoisie he found frankly boring. Thanks to a very good memory, he passed his examinations, but his student years were devoted mainly to pleasure: theater, races, cafés, and parties. He cared so little for the common run of success that once he had passed his qualifying examinations he didn't bother to present a thesis but registered himself in the Court of Appeals and took a post as secretary to a well-established lawyer. He was contemptuous of successes which are obtained at the expense of hard work and effort; according to him, if you were "born" to be someone, you automatically possessed all the essential qualities—wit, talent, charm, and good breeding. The trouble was that in the ranks of that high society to which he laid claim for admittance, he found he was a nobody: the *de* in "de Beauvoir" showed he had a handle to his name, but the name was an obscure one, and did not automatically open the doors of the best clubs and the most aristocratic salons: and he hadn't the means to live like a lord. He attached little importance to the positions that were open to him in the bourgeois world—the distinguished lawyer, the father of a family, the respected citizen. He set out in life with empty hands, and despised the advantages he acquired. There was only one solution left to him: to become an actor. . . . (36)

To remedy the lack of satisfaction in real distinction, the only way out seemed what the memorialist calls *paraître* (appearance), a desire curiously close to the hasty answer the young André Gide once gave when, at the famous five o'clock at Mallarmé's, he was asked what was his "formula": "représenter"—which Gide immediately came to regret. Despite Georges de Beauvoir's fondness for the stage, he never once thought of defying the prejudices of his environment and becoming an actor for good. Amateurism helped him preserve just enough drive to satisfy his need for prestige, and on the other hand, the legal profession more or less guaranteed his status.

Simone's mother, Françoise, was born in Verdun "in a rich and devout bourgeois family"(40). Françoise's father was a banker who had been educated by Jesuits. Her mother had received her education in a convent. Françoise suffered from the rather distant affection of her mother, while her father preferred his younger daughter to her. She was a day student at the Couvent des Oiseaux. Though an attractive young woman, she had so little self-assurance that she was, in her daughter's eyes, always watching what others did in order to know how to behave. Despite certain rigid prejudices, she managed to live in harmony with a husband who in many respects disagreed with her ideals.

Françoise de Beauvoir was a devout Catholic, while Georges never concealed his scepticism:

he was an unbeliever. This scepticism did not affect me, so deeply did I feel myself penetrated by the presence of God; yet Papa was always right: how could he be mistaken about the most obvious of all truths? Nevertheless, since my mother, who was so pious, seemed to find Papa's attitude quite natural, I accepted it calmly. The consequence was that I grew accustomed to the idea that my intellectual life—embodied by my father—and my spiritual life—expressed by my mother—were two radically incongruous fields of experience which had absolutely nothing in common. . . . So I set God apart from life and the world, and this attitude was to have a profound influence on my future development. (44)

II   *The Seeds of Rebellion Against Women's Condition*

Her earliest memories show Simone as a cheerful little girl. However, when she became upset, she would go into fits, between the age of three and a half and five years. In her sober, humorous way, she describes her kicking and screaming younger self. Sharply distrustful of "false" gestures, she refused to cooperate: "As soon as I ever suspected, rightly or wrongly, that people were taking advantage of my ingenuousness in order to get me to do something, my gorge rose and I began to kick out in all directions" (16). Much in the same vein, as soon as she became suspicious of the Christmas "miracle," she challenged her parents, who "confessed." What stupefied Simone was the possibility of there being "false certainties." This paradox stems from an earlier disposition that the mature writer attempts to define as a revolt against what the translator—on the whole quite competent—has rendered as her "youthful state" ("ma condition enfantine") (17). The French version evokes more clearly the author's lifelong struggle for the rights of the individual, against suppression of the rights of children as well as women.

In passing, also, she reminisces on the "black magic of words" (22). In view of Sartre's evocation of his youth in much the same mood, this is a significant meeting of minds that have so much else in common. It was at a very early age that the child discovered the beauty of nature, another lifelong passion. Simone de Beauvoir also excels in depicting the self-centered little saint she was at the age of six, at the outbreak of the First World War, when she shared in the nationalist fervor.

While admiring her father for his intellectual and artistic accomplishments, the young girl never spoke to him. Her mother's role was different. More of an authoritarian, she nonetheless was open to requests to a degree that at times amazed her daughter. Simone's younger sister helped her live through the sterner days of childhood. Thanks to Hélène, whom they called Poupette, "I got into the habit of wanting to communicate with people" (47).

Like thousands of Catholic mothers, Madame de Beauvoir selected the reading material for her daughters. This was done from the time when Simone had just begun to read up through her high school years. In spite of this limitation on her choice of books, Simone enjoyed reading to an extraordinary extent. Her imagination was stimulated by what she read, and she manifested great sensitivity in her reactions. Reading, playing with other children, spending her vacations at the family mansion in the Limousin, Simone grew up happily. She notes that she had no regret at being a girl, a statement that must come as a surprise to readers of *The Second Sex*.

Simone was a pious child. She regularly went to confession and to communion. Hers was the typical protected childhood of a middle-

class girl in the early years of this century, unaware of "indecent"
language and books. "While I chafed at restraints imposed by other
people's wills, I felt no resentment at those inflicted on me by things
like the weather"—a translation which blurs the author's thought:
"que m'imposaient les choses" (85). She formed the most important
friendship of her youth when she was about to turn ten: Elisabeth
Mabille—"Zaza"—became her classmate, and at once there developed a close and deep relationship. At the age of eleven, Simone
visualized herself as "hors série": "I was convinced that I would be,
that I was already, one in a million" (96). This thought demonstrates
her determination to get ahead in life and be someone. At the same
time, she readily admits her manners were "awkward," especially in
comparison to the far more spontaneous Zaza (98). It was also at this
time, when she was eleven, that the writer notes that she was
"opposed to marriage and motherhood." That was to become one of
the themes of her life and work. Among the books she devoured,
Louisa May Alcott's *Little Women* is noted as having had a
very special influence. The imagination of the young reader was
fired by the adventures of the March sisters, and often enough
young Simone viewed herself as Jo or another of the Alcott heroines.

The conservative education of girls prevented Simone from an-
ticipating the physiological changes of puberty. When the shock of
menstruation occurred, the girl passed through contradictory emotions, from fright and shame to a kind of pride, as her mother
seemed to consider her having joined the sisterhood of women. But
her father apparently was not above teasing her about the newly
acquired sign of maturity, which she resented to the point of being
consumed with shame: "I was horrified at the thought that he suddenly considered me to be a mere organism"; and she adds: "Je me
sentis à jamais déchue" (which is translated as: "I felt as if I could
never hold up my head again" [107]). This impression was to become the first impulse for, if not the nucleus of, the idea of *The
Second Sex*, where the writer would discuss woman's "contingency"
and "immanence."

Observing the daily routine of cooking, washing dishes, and piling
dishes in the kitchen cabinet, over and over again, young Simone
wondered whether she, too, was to waste her life endlessly on such
futile chores. "Could I live like that," she asks (110). The later
antibourgeois stance adopted by Simone de Beauvoir stems from

thoughts of that kind. That is why her memoirs are an inexhaust-
ible source for all who wish to follow the development of a truly
free mind. Even if we remain sceptical as to the chronological accuracy of such notations, no one could doubt their fundamental
veracity.

Besides criticizing, at least mentally, the general conditions of
middle class life, already at this early stage, the young girl also
watched her own parents and their relationship with one another
with a critical eye. She finds her mother to be but an imperfect
"accomplice" of her father and one who tries only "timid revolts."
This was the time when Simone ceased to believe her father infalli-
ble and when she learned "how to be secretive" (115) at the age of
twelve.

As she tackled more mature books, her mind gained firmness; she
"emancipated" herself somewhat, breaking free "from the bonds of
childhood" (116). Thanks to Zaza's influence and determined attitude, Simone increasingly learned how to use her mind. Thus,
Zaza's cynicism helped open Simone's eyes in religious matters:
"she never made fun of my faults, only of my virtues" (123). Yet, the
"dutiful daughter" could not accomplish this progress without hesitation. At the same time, she learned to size up the teachers at the
Cours Désir; even her father called them "a little backward" (129).

III Doubts

While Simone and Zaza are gradually freeing themselves, their
mothers are still opening, and reading first, the letters they exchange. The description of the intimate thoughts and feelings of the
young teenager in the throes of religious doubts has great honesty
and real beauty. God was felt to be much more close and real in the
countryside than in Paris, and the struggle in Simone's heart and
mind was protracted. What helped her to solve the problem little by
little was her boundless curiosity about the secrets of life and nature
as she could observe their interplay in the country. Her increasingly
independent mind very soon saw through the "sectarian teaching"
she was offered. Naturally, the indoctrination at the Cours Désir
was rather unsophisticated, and in the case of Simone the results
were diametrically opposed to those anticipated. Almost all of the
more substantial studies on her, written by French Catholics, dwell
at great length on the problem of her education, trying to explain

the "apostasy." Father Henry accuses both her parents of having been indifferent in their belief; the mother, he claims, with all her staunchly devout attitude, was unable to "inspire" her daughters. The father, universally called a "sceptic," was a political and moral conservative who limited his critical remarks to the foibles of religious life and education. And the parochial schools, despite their zeal and virtue, did not know how to cope with an exceptionally bright pupil and her questions of conscience; confession and communion, instead of bringing the child closer to her advisers, had the reverse effects.

Georges de Beauvoir prophesied somber future struggles, predicting the triumph of the "barbarians." But Simone had found a position from which she could view such dire prognostications with equanimity: "Whatever happens . . . it will be men [meaning human beings] who win the final victory" (136), a beautiful illustration of her early disposition to true humanism, her later scorn for the term notwithstanding. Her father belittled the justification of social demands: workers had no right to be dissatisfied, in his view. He would shrug his shoulders and declare emphatically: "they're not dying of starvation . . . " (138).

It is hardly necessary to point out that such opinions could not remain unchallenged in the mind of his daughter, whose sensitivity to inequities had developed from childhood. If, today, she has assumed a leading position in political and social matters for which she is known throughout the world, it is in large part owing to the provocative nature of prejudiced pronouncements in her immediate environment as a child and adolescent. Having learned to discern between the conflicting versions given of society by her father and in books and treatises that she would pore over, Simone had to overcome the point of view of her own class in order to find herself and to make her voice heard in a plea for human dignity. Once that position was clear, she would never deviate from it. Without partisan dogmatism, lucidly and firmly, she would show the way to improvement and progress as she saw them.

Several moments in the life of the Catholic girl of the Parisian middle class were to determine her personality. Very early in life, she was to find herself at odds with her confessor. Father Martin's use of a protective, condescending tone toward children led Simone, who was then fourteen, to rebel against his authority. He started his mild-sounding admonition by saying:

It has come to my ears that my little Simone has changed . . . that she is disobedient, noisy, that she answers back when she is reprimanded. From now on you must be careful about these things.

My cheeks were ablaze, I gazed with horror upon the impostor whom for years I had taken as the representative of God on earth; it was as if he had suddenly tucked up his cassock and revealed the skirts of an old religious bigot; the priest's robe was only a disguise; it covered an old busybody [une commère qui se repaissait de ragots] who fed on gossip. (142)

If God "emerged blameless" ("indemne") from this episode, the first crack had appeared in the hitherto solid wall of her faith. From that time on, Simone observed her surroundings with an increasingly critical eye. She was to discover other flaws. So it was "with no great surprise" that she told herself one day, "I no longer believe in God." And she reasoned:

That was proof: if I had believed in Him, I should not have allowed myself to offend Him so lightheartedly. I had always thought that the world was a small price to pay for eternity; but it was worth more than that, because I loved the world, and it was suddenly God whose price was small [qui ne faisait pas le poids]: from now on His name would have to be a cover for nothing more than a mirage. For a long time now the concept that I had of Him had been purified and refined, sublimated to the point where He was faceless. He no longer had any concrete link with the earth, or therefore any being. His perfection canceled out His reality. That is why I felt so little surprise when I became aware of His absence in my heart and in heaven. I was not denying Him in order to rid myself of an intruder: on the contrary, I realized that He was playing no further part in my life, and so I concluded that He had ceased to exist for me. (144–45)

In this and subsequent passages, the strict consistency of her development is noted with scrupulous honesty. Not a word in excess is used to register, in plausible order, the events that must have led to so essential a clarity. She argues that her father's scepticism had shown her the way; hence she did not choose an absolutely lonely path nor a wildly adventurous one. She sensed an immense relief in finding herself freed "from her childhood and her sex" and in agreement with the free thinkers she admired. It was easier for her to think of "a world without a creator than of a creator burdened with all the contradictions of the world" (145). And, she adds, "my incredulity never once wavered."

Her explanation is given without aggressive overtones of arrogance or overconfidence. There is certainly some regret to be found—and found openly, not between the lines; not so much the loss of faith in itself is deplored as the necessity to cut herself off completely from the trends of thought familiar to her, as well as to her friends. The clinical sobriety of her findings has shocked some critics, who would have preferred to see her moan over the loss of certainties. But if the reader will apply standards of simple good faith, he can compare those pages in their simplicity to the passages about her early childhood where Simone de Beauvoir already had exposed "false certainties" and the world of make-believe. She does not turn against her own past, but she denounces the weaknesses and fallacies of bourgeois morality, the hypocrisy of conformity. Nowhere in her work is there any mockery of religion. The only indictment resulting from her account of her youth is that against falsehood and bigotry.

IV *The Realization of Mortality*

Another fundamental revelation the very young girl was to experience proved to be the discovery that she was "condemned to death" (146). The haunting presence of death, a theme found in so many works of art and literature the world over, has remained a reality throughout Simone de Beauvoir's work as well. A systematic study of the theme has been superbly done by Elaine Marks (*Simone de Beauvoir: Encounter with Death*, New Brunswick, Rutgers University Press, 1973). The concern with death has more prominence in some of Simone de Beauvoir's books than in others. *L'Invitée (She Came to Stay)*, *Les Bouches inutiles*, *Le Sang des autres (The Blood of Others)*, and *Tous les Hommes sont mortels (All Men Are Mortal)*, are all dominated by the shadow of death, while in *Les Mandarins (The Mandarins)* and in *Les Belles Images* death is no more than an incidental occurrence of passing importance, although there, too, a few of the characters will muse on mortality. And, of course, her memoirs are full of references to the progress of the idea of death in her mind, while a whole volume of her autobiographical writings is devoted entirely to this crucial question—*Une Mort très douce (A Very Easy Death)*.

The first encounter with the idea of death is recalled from her childhood; Simone may have been thirteen or fourteen years old when she first screamed and rebeled against her mortal condition. She then asked herself: "How do other people manage? How shall *I* manage?" (146); it seemed impossible to her, then, to live "with

such horror gnawing at my heart." "Even more than death itself,"
she remarks, "I feared that terror which would soon be with me
always" (146). Years later, a similarly striking experience is noted.
Aged twenty-one, Simone admits: "The fear of death had never left
me, I couldn't get used to the thought; I would still sometimes shake
and weep with terror. . ." (281). But the description of such terror
alternates in her memoirs with scenes of gay youthful adventures, of
discoveries, of sound curiosity about people, places, and things.

Many of these events are recounted with the finest, subtlest
humor, often applied to her own attitudes and feelings in retrospect.
That is what makes the volumes of memoirs such a rich and
trustworthy source of information. It cannot be stated too emphatically that Simone de Beauvoir enables the readers to know her well,
quite to the contrary of so many writers of memoirs and diaries, who
seem interested above all else in the impression they create of
themselves. On the other hand, we may sometimes be shocked by
the reckless way in which incidents are evoked, involving prominent people—or just plain people for that matter—whose weaknesses are unveiled or ridiculed. Yet, since the writer does not
exempt herself from such harsh and realistic exposure, we must, on
the whole, acknowledge her fundamental good faith and a degree of
sincerity rare in any period. Compared to her openness and complete lack of "pose," Gide's famous "sincerity" leaves an aftertaste of
the cosmetic.

The style of her memoirs is a mixture of matter of factness and
analytical prose such as we see in her essays and of beautiful, sometimes poetic, formulae. For an author who tends to be exceedingly
casual, to the point of clumsiness and neglect of elementary rules of
style, it is surprising to find so many pages ringing with the music of
true emotion, conveying the poignancy of her experience.

As for the writer's curiosity in people mentioned above, an
episode which occurred early in her life may be considered
paradigmatic. Given permission to stay up late while her father
went out to play bridge, her mother and sister having gone to bed,
Simone would get her father's opera glasses and spy on the lives of
strangers, "conscious of the fascination of these little peep shows,
these lighted rooms suspended in the night" (164). Often in real life,
as well as in fictional situations, Simone de Beauvoir practiced this
occupation of the spectator, although not so often in as voyeuristic a
manner as in her adolescence. It may explain the freshness of her

views, the genuine interest her characters evoke, the correct interpretation of social or psychological phenomena. Again, the mature writer shows no petty or morbid curiosity either about herself or about her fictional characters. The memoirs show us one instance of a natural, spontaneous, juvenile impulse when at nineteen, at the country place of her friend Zaza, she came across the open diary of Geneviève de Bréville, who had just written in the journal that Simone was to arrive the next day, adding that she got no gratification out of that visit since she did not like her.

Gide's protagonists, on the other hand, are often driven to commit acts of extreme indiscretion, as in *Les Caves du Vatican (Lafcadio's Adventures)* or *Les Faux-Monnayeurs (The Counterfeiters)*, where such acts border on the morbid. Frankly curious about the way people live in different parts of the world, the adult Simone de Beauvoir set out on long expeditions into Africa, North and South America, and China, among other countries, to bring back her subjective but often novel impressions. In Paris, the street cafés afforded her the ideal observatory from which to study her contemporaries. She gleaned such observations for use in both her fiction and her essays.

V *Why Philosophy?*

The thing that attracted me about philosophy was that it went straight to essentials. I had never liked fiddling with detail: I perceived the general significance of things rather than their singularities, and I preferred understanding to seeing; I had always wanted to know *everything;* philosophy would allow me to satisfy this desire, for it aimed at total reality; philosophy went right to the heart of truth and revealed to me, instead of an illusory whirlwind of facts or empirical laws, an order, a reason, a necessity in everything. The sciences, literature, and all other disciplines seemed to me to be very poor relations to philosophy (167).

This statement, made at about the time she was to pass her examination for the baccalauréat, stands in sharp contradiction with another one, somewhat later but quite typical and constant in her life: she preferred literature to philosophy and wrote that she would not have been pleased at all if people had told her that she was to become a sort of Bergson. The contradiction, however, is more apparent than real, as Simone would amalgamate in her thought elements of the two worlds that, after all, cannot be separated so neatly.

Just as conditions had radically changed from what they had been before 1914, so they have changed since the days of Simone de Beauvoir's teens when she found out that "appearances were deceptive and the world I had been taught to believe in was a pack of lies"(173). These remarks refer to the particularly ludicrous lack of candor in matters of sex education, or rather, the complete absence of such education. The memoir writer contrasts her observations of general insincerity with her ideal view of love: it was to be all or nothing, even though she had not pondered the portent of such a claim. In the first volume of memoirs, the absolute proclamation of her ideal is made to sound amusing, precisely in view of accepted standards of morality. Thus, her book becomes a clue to the deficiencies not just of her own caste and world, but of morality in bourgeois society altogether, as *The Second Sex* eventually became an act of accusation against the perpetuation of taboos and of prejudice concerning women.

Very early, Simone became conscious of what made her different from other girls. While her way of describing this awareness may sound a bit arrogant, we should not forget that she was tracing her own evolution for all to see, much in the vein that Montaigne used his own example. Had she chosen to remain silent on this essential moment in her life, the reader would have been rightly disappointed at the lack of psychological—or simply logical—depth. What makes this writer different from others does indeed belong in her autobiography.

Therefore, it is indispensable to note the stages of her intellectual formation as they are depicted for us to see. Coming back from an interview with her former teacher, Garric, [not the founder of *L'Action Française,* as some hasty biographer would have it] in a scene both simple and highly dramatic, Simone de Beauvoir utters the solemn vow that her life must be useful, that everything in her life must be of service to mankind. This vow is all the more remarkable, as the difficulties encountered on her path were many and manifested themselves early. In deciding on the career of a teacher, she realized full well how lonely she would be: "even if I were to form one or two friendships, they would never console me for the sense of exile I was already beginning to feel; I had always been . . . looked upon as the center of excited comment; I loved being loved: the bleakness of my future terrified me"(200).

The choice of a career, not yet generally accepted for girls in the nineteen twenties, was imposed upon her by her family situation. Her father bluntly declared that, in the absence of a dowry, his daughters would have to work, and thereby meant to announce a lamentable fate which, to Simone's ears, did not sound devastating at all. Difficulties arose when she first realized how many obstacles were added to the normal roadblocks due to the uncompromising nature of her mind. It should be borne in mind that Catholic families in those days considered teaching in state schools near treason. Faced with the necessity of pursuing her way without alienating her parents, with whose moral judgements she disagreed, she chose to remain silent. Her silence was rightly interpreted as a protest. Some of her attitudes are reflected in the fragments the author allows us to see of her earlier attempts at fiction. Her statement that "Through the character of Eliane I described myself . . ." culminates in a typical challenge to the others: "She felt sufficiently strong in herself to defend her one possession against blows and blandishments, and to keep her fist tightly closed all the time" (203).

Such proud self-reliance—if one may call it that—and refusal to communicate recall a similar pronouncement made over two centuries earlier by Fontenelle; the pioneer of philosophic thought had shown his pessimism when he said: "Had I my hand full of truths, I would take good care not to divulge them."[2] Simone, on the other hand, was silent only toward those who reasoned with her and tried to mollify her resolve. Her mother best sensed this pride when she said: "Simone would rather bite her tongue out than say what she is thinking," a statement rather less forceful in translation than the original: "Simone aimerait mieux se mettre toute nue que de dire ce qu'elle a dans la tête" (203).

Silence did not solve the problem of Simone's difficult relations with her parents. Feeling "cornered," she tried to "put on a protective armor by exhorting [her]self not to be afraid of blame, ridicule, or lack of understanding" (204). Since she felt confronted by what she saw as universal lies, her one escape was in reading books by authors who explicitly espoused the causes she believed in. Here, Gide's famous imprecation, "Family, I hate you . . . ," comforted her, and books for a while became her only allies. Among her readings, we may note the recurrent stress on Alain-Fournier's *The Wanderer*, the first reading of which brought tears to her eyes. But above all she acknowledged intellectual affinities with writers who had made the break with the bourgeois past. At the ages of sixteen and seventeen, she read "feverishly all the novels, all the essays of my older contemporaries" (205)—a translation which falls short of ". . . de mes jeunes aínés"—Barrès (!), Gide, Valéry, Claudel. "Bourgeois like myself, they too felt ill at ease and out of place."

Together with such reading, Simone's attitude toward her parents helped shape her personality. The theme of "otherness" may have come already into the picture: "I would gaze in the looking glass at the person *they* could see: it wasn't *me;* I wasn't there, I wasn't anywhere . . ." (204).

The depth of her rebellious feeling is hard to assess, but we must not forget that her resentment often enough is based on real personal knowledge of narrow-mindedness in her environment. As she put it: "Since childhood I had been questing for absolute sincerity. All around me people deplored falsehood, but were careful to avoid the truth" (206).

Having passed from the protected environment of the Cours Désir to the Institut Sainte-Marie, directed by Madame Daniélou, a school recommended by Zaza's father in order to minimize the effect of the Sorbonne teachings on his daughter and Simone, the young future teacher felt somewhat encouraged in her desire for more independence. She found certain courses quite stimulating, especially the classes of Mademoiselle Lambert. Her sharp eye for weaknesses in her teachers was compensated by her ability to appreciate genuine intelligence. Above all, she prized Garric's lectures, which inspired her to improve her mind in every way. Thus, while she increasingly resented her dependence on her parents and felt frustrated by the material aspects of that situation, philosophy appeared to her the most satisfying study. At the same time, following the trend set by the institut, she volunteered to participate in social service groups.

At this time, her deep love of nature, which plays a vital role in her life, was a source of strength, replacing in part, no doubt, her religious feeling of belonging. The only time when she was completely at ease was during long walks in the countryside. Without lyricism, but with a good firm pace, she set out on the lifelong exploration of nature as an antidote against the disappointment of people and circumstances.

The depth of her resentment of society, and in particular of those close to her, may seem quite shocking. Yet we must not neglect taking into account the equally biting self-criticism she practiced all along, and everywhere, in all her memoirs. One example will suffice: "My poverty and helplessness would have worried me less if I had had the least suspicion of how ignorant and narrow-minded I still was. . . ." (242). One should note, however, that the resentment shown by Simone was partially nourished by her sensitivity to the growing vulgarity demonstrated by her father. Though she readily recognized that he had been ruined by the war, that all his illusions had been swept away, the loudness of his tone in public places embarrassed his daughter. Whereas he always professed to esteem courtesy, he now "outcommoned the common" and "succeeded so well in appearing to be a nonentity that in the end no one but himself could be expected to know he was anything else" (187).

Trying to explain a certain change of her intellectual allegiance, Simone lucidly describes her state of mind at the time when, under the influence of her cousin Jacques, she "abandoned Gide and Barrès" and searched for other models. It was at this stage that she underwent the purely philosophical temptation of suicide. Her passionate love of life helped her overcome this crisis, a love often stated in terms of courage by a writer who never cast herself in the role of a heroine.

Simone's feelings for her cousin Jacques were ambivalent throughout the years of her adolescence. Inexperienced in matters of the heart, she took his gentle, winning ways for genuine affection, and indeed, Jacques liked his little cousin well enough. At times, she felt left out when he confided in friends, oblivious of her presence. At other times, when he was depressed over an examination failure, over his eventual *embourgeoisement*, he would let himself be comforted by Simone. Their family, too, contributed to the ambiguity of their situation. Her grandfather had refused to envisage a marriage between the two young people—even though the word marriage or the very idea had never been hinted openly—while Simone's parents viewed such a union with obvious favor for financial reasons. Her own emotions fluctuated: "he loves me, he is indifferent . . . ." She also realized that her independence as a professional woman would be jeopardized in such a marriage. Nowhere are these alternating moods stated better than in a notation in her diary, written when Simone was nineteen: "It's when I feel I love him most that I hate all the more the love I have for him."

Relating the episode, she adds: "I was afraid that my affection for
him would trap me into becoming his wife, and I savagely rejected
the sort of life that awaited the future Madame Laiguillon*" (246).
It was at this time, too, that she met left-wing intellectuals. They
exercised a great fascination over her, though they had no overwhelming impact on her thinking. Her conversations with them,
however, opened her mind to new truths and "evidences." In retrospect, she pictures herself as still undecided, *fumeuse* (i.e.,
hazy), but she knew she loathed right-wing extremists and their
brutal, coarse, and shallow activities. Right-wing ideology represented what was worst in her own class. Since her father had
shown uncritical acceptance of all the most tired cliches of
chauvinism, Simone had had early warnings, making her exceptionally alert against the fallacies of nationalism.

At the same time that she became acquainted with new ideas in
politics, Simone at nineteen struck up friendships that were to determine her course in life. She sharpened her mind in banter as well
as in serious talk with Pradelle*. Her friendship with Zaza had freed
Simone from a number of taboos: belonging to a family comparable
in background with Simone's, Zaza was both firm in her religious
beliefs and emancipated from many of the uncertainties and
timidities that still inhibited her friend. A "dutiful daughter" too,
Zaza knew how to combine a respectful love for her mother and
independence of mind and conscience. A proof of this independence
can be seen in her steadfast friendship with Simone, a friendship
which her mother actually attempted to disrupt at any cost.

Musing on her own merits and shortcomings, Simone wondered
whether "men marry women like me." She concluded: "What was
cutting me off from other people was a certain violence of temperament which only I seemed to possess" (261). Hence she thought her
lot would be loneliness, a theme frequently aired in later years,
sometimes with a feeling of pride, at other moments with sadness.
To overcome this feeling of isolation, she set out to write a "vast
novel," but when she discovered she had nothing of substance to
tell, being so inexperienced in life, she shelved her project. Draw-
ing up a plan for her studies, she took pleasure in "planning [her]
future in detail"—("mettre l'avenir en fiches") (273).

To the reader of the memoirs, the intellectual atmosphere of the
late twenties comes to life, as we are shown how Simone, attracted
at the same time by philosophy and by Surrealism, was largely

untouched by marxist preachings, yet aware of the need for social change. Like a female Rastignac, Simone de Beauvoir confronts life and accepts its challenge. Her adult sense of humor puts in perspective the elation felt when she was praised by her professor for an essay: " 'I became swelled-headed. I am sure that I shall reach loftier heights than any of them. Is this pride? If I didn't have genius, it would be; but if I *have* got genius—as I sometimes believe; as I am sometimes *quite sure*—then it simply means that I clearly recognize my superior gifts,' I wrote complacently in my diary" (280). Such candor in revealing juvenile flights of one's own ambition is surely extremely rare.

At the same time as she itches intellectually, so to speak, her innate curiosity impels her to explore Paris nightlife, of which she had only the vaguest notions. What is so refreshing in the perilous adventures she induced her younger sister to share with her is the complete innocence of these expeditions. Naive to a point hard to imagine for a girl who grew up in Paris—and yet this naivete was by no means exceptional—she plunged into the nightspots like an explorer into a cavern. She went into bars and nightclubs in the candid hope of experiencing sensations she could not even anticipate; but despite her daring, nothing untoward happened. The nostalgia for the Jockey Club and other places of revelry remained with her for many years, even though she soon saw through the mock air of sophisticated urbanity and supposed vice.

Some of her forays into the streets and cafes of Paris were not without problems. Playing with fire, the inexperienced, innocent girl exposed herself to many embarrassing situations but again escaped unharmed and with a sense of having achieved something: an excursion into the dangerous real world, seen at times as a gratuitous act precisely on account of the danger involved. Such foolhardy pranks may surprise in someone as intellectually precocious as Simone de Beauvoir. The thought of these escapades later filled her "with disgust" (307), which did not prevent her from returning to the places of her erstwhile exploits. Failing to renew the old excitement in revisiting her former haunts, she notes in her diary, no doubt with an exaggerated expression of wonderment: "Jazz, loose women, sexy dancing, bad words, drink, physical intimacies: how is it I'm not shocked, but willingly accept, and bandy lewd expressions with strange men? How does it happen that I like these things, have such an incongruous passion for them; and why does this passion have such a strong hold over me? What am I looking for in these places with their curious, dubious charm?" (326).

No answer is given to these questions; yet the memorialist's frank admission of youthful impulses shows clearly that no actual perversion had occurred in her: she remained untouched by the temptations of vice, and her mind was intact. Judging without weakness what had been an aberration, she records almost impartially the meanderings of her younger self in search of its identity. The frivolousness of her nocturnal adventures must have been the ransom paid for a long succession of frustrations and of taboos. Trite though these explorations of a corner of the adult world would appear, they fit into the curious rhythm observed in her development, where outright rebellion against parental authority alternates with loyal, though ultimately futile, attempts at adjustment to society and her class, if not to her own family. A sense of mission appears in the very challenge the young student feels facing her, and it causes her not to yield on essential points.

Such a militant disposition by no means always prevailed: indeed, Simone often acquiesced in her parents' demands when she did not feel her private domain was being intruded upon. An exaltation filled her when, one spring she embarked on the spur of the moment, without "even a toothbrush," on a chance trip by train with her father to the familiar mansion of her aunt, which she had known only during the summers, That exaltation exactly duplicated one she had felt shortly before that trip when, on the way to the country house of her friend Zaza's parents, she also had enjoyed the freedom and motion of the train: "I loved trains. Leanout of the window, I surrendered my face to the wind and the flying cinders and swore never to be like travelers who always huddle together in the stuffiness of their compartments" (268). This mood accurately reflects the one voiced by the German Romantic poet Eichendorff, whose famous Good-for-Nothing rejoiced in the freedom of the open road on early mornings, deriding the "lazy people in their beds whom down does not refresh."[3]

Through tensions and clashes, her attitude toward philosophy necessarily changed. At one time, philosophy was a bulwark against the religious temptation; at other moments, its strict discipline and rigors could not fulfill her demands for prompt solutions in her own life. "Reading a book on Kant, I developed a passion for critical idealism which confirmed me in my rejection of God. In Bergson's theories about 'the social ego and the personal ego,' I enthusiastically recognized my own experience. But the impersonal voices of the philosophers didn't bring me the same consolation as those of favorite authors . . . " (219). Yet, the age-old Voltairian questions on the "why," "whence," and "how" of existence persist in Simone's mind, and she anxiously questions literature, science, and all other disciplines open to her, integrating her findings into her experience of daily living: "I began by groping my way blindly through the system of Descartes and Spinoza. These sometimes bore me to lofty heights out into the infinite: I would see the earth like an ant hill at my feet. . . . Sometimes they seemed no more than clumsy scaffoldings constructed in air without any relationship to reality . . . " (235). Even Kant, in whose works she found strong support for her own social ideas, failed to explain the mystery of the universe and of her own existence.

But regardless of all the disappointing and conventional teachings, philosophy was nevertheless worth studying in earnest: "Philosophy had neither opened the heavens to me, nor anchored me to earth; all the same, . . . when I had mastered the first difficulties, I began to take a serious interest in it. . . " (247). After reading some major philosophical treatises, she became certain that this was the road to wisdom. Some time later, however, in the midst of a routine of teaching and studying, appeasing her parents' worry about her salvation, she declared herself "satiated with philosophy" (287).

This statement, made at twenty, recalls one that is quite typical and constant in her life. In connection with this pure speculation about what never was to be, we should be allowed a glimpse into the future as it is recorded in the second volume of the memoirs, where similar attitudes toward philosophy are reflected. In 1935, Simone recalls, when she was reluctant to tackle philosophy, Sartre "had declared that [her] grasp of philosophical doctrines, including that held by Husserl, was quicker and more precise than his own." It should be borne in mind that Sartre was trying to encourage her when she hesitated to try her hand at philosophical writing. Also, Simone sees clearly that

he tended to interpret [these philosophical doctrines] according to his own hypotheses; he found great difficulty in jettisoning his own viewpoint and unreservedly adopting anyone else's. In my case, there was no such resistance to break down: my thinking bent itself directly to the point I was attempting to master. I did not, however, accept it passively: the degree of my acceptance was always modified by the lacunae and muddled logic I perceived in any proposition . . . ."[4]

An independent mind endowed with a growing sense of intellectual responsibility, Simone de Beauvoir is able to analyze her capacity of thinking in philosophical terms, of delineating theory and doctrine, of sizing up paradox and constructive theorems. In the context of the 1935 discussion, she continues to describe the functioning of her acumen: "If a theory convinced me, it did not remain an external, alien phenomenon; it altered my relationship with the world, and colored all my experience. In short, I possessed both considerable powers of assimilation and a well-developed critical sense; and philosophy was for me a living reality, which gave me never-failing satisfaction" (*Prime*, 178).

While asserting her competence, rationally and with no undue claim to superiority, Simone de Beauvoir remains capable of perceiving the natural limitations of her mind, as she states, still in the same passage of her second volume of memoirs, that she did not regard herself as a philosopher, a view well in line with judgements she made much later and quite emphatically on the whole of her work. That is why, in this study, the space allocated to her philosophical essays will be limited, in keeping also with the general opinion of serious critics. As to her reasons for not regarding herself as a philosopher, they are many; chief among them is that, as she declares: "I was well aware that the ease with which I penetrated to the heart of a text stemmed, precisely, from my lack of originality" (*Prime*, 178). She goes on to show that only certain individuals, an elite, are "capable of getting results from the conscious venture into lunacy known as a 'philosophical system,' from which they derive that obsessional attitude which endows their tentative patterns with universal insight and applicability" (178). She concludes by saying that "women are not by nature prone to obsessions of this type" (178). This statement, repeating earlier views on the subject, will have to be discussed more thoroughly in the context of the author's study of women's condition in *The Second Sex*, although it might be noted here that the translator's choice of "obsession" for "obstination" is open to debate.

Whereas Simone had found herself well-equipped to confront the problems of philosophical study, her memoirs allow us to follow the arduous path she was treading through the labyrinthine paths of philosophy. During the German Occupation, she went to the Bibliothèque Nationale to read Hegel's *Phenomenology of Mind*, and noted "at present, can scarcely make head or tail of a word of it" (*Prime*, 363). This was the first such notation, followed by similar ones, the next few days. It was not until some time later, after considerable struggle with the text, that she could understand Hegel better. "His amplitude of detail dazzled me, and his system as a whole made me feel giddy . . ." (372).

While borrowing from a passage by Hegel the motto to be used for the epigraph of *She Came to Stay*, Simone steeped herself in much of Hegel's phenomenology. Yet, after some initial approval of his system, she parted company with him, ready to affirm a more positive concept of mankind: "The further I went, the more I diverged from Hegel, without ever losing my admiration for him. I knew already that in the very marrow of my being I was bound up with my contemporaries; now I was learning that this dependent condition carried a complementary burden of responsibility" (373). An examination of the scope of Simone de Beauvoir's contribution to the enunciation of Existentialism will be attempted in the section devoted to her essay on the subject. Quite aside from philosophical essays, however, what makes this writer a champion of Existentialism is the totality of her writings. Even as late as 1943, when Jean Grenier asked her whether she was an existentialist, Simone de Beauvoir showed embarrassment at this question, mainly on account of her congenital self-effacing attitude:

I had read Kierkegaard, and the term "existential philosophy" had been in circulation for some time apropos of Heidegger; but I didn't understand the meaning of the word "existentialist," which Gabriel Marcel had recently coined. Besides, Grenier's question clashed with my modesty and my pride alike. I was not of sufficient importance, objectively considered, to merit any such label; as for my ideas, I was convinced that they reflected the truth rather than some entrenched doctrinal position. . . . (433)

Out of a great many pronouncements on philosophy and philosophical doctrines, these few words suffice to demonstrate the varying degrees of involvement that Simone de Beauvoir went through in her development. As she ended up by keeping a less

strict separation between her fiction and her essays and by implicitly
stating quite a few philosophical themes, the early struggle in her
mind is apt to show with uncanny clarity both her firm determination as a creative writer and the solid basis of her thought.

VI End of Old Attachments, Beginning of the New

Simone's friends knew one another, when she was twenty, and
they went out in a large group to revisit old haunts like the Jockey.
Thus it came about that Zara and Pradelle* grew close to each other,
with Simone being very happy over her friends' finding happiness—a happiness of sorts, as it developed. For Pradelle, charming
and sincere though he was, hesitated, while Zaza had to fight every
inch of the way with her mother, who wanted to lay down the
age-old family rule and marry off her daughter to some wealthy
man. The dramatic end of Zaza's life is told with moving,
breathtaking simplicity. A violent fever developed within a few
days. The author leaves it undecided whether the extreme emotional pressure that Zaza was subjected to had anything to do with
her death or whether it was a clinical case. The first volume of
memoirs ends with the words: "for a long time I believed that I had
paid for my own freedom with her death" (Memoirs, 382).

The freedom she achieved was clearly not bought at that price,
not objectively at least. Through Herbaud*, one of her prestigious
fellow students and fellow candidates for the Agrégation, Simone
had found a rare friendship that stimulated her intellectually and
finished emancipating her from her old environment. For a time
Herbaud, while a true friend, kept her from meeting his other close
friends, Sartre and Nizan. Only when the others—Sartre, Nizan,
and Simone—succeeded at the Agrégation, while he himself failed
and had to leave Paris, did Simone get closer to Sartre.

Herbaud had told Simone of many of Sartre's qualities, among
them an unexpected sense of humor. Sartre excelled in every farce
and grotesque college comedy: he was the star of the Ecole Nor-
male. He also generously helped his "petits camarades," as the clan
was baptized, prepare the orals of the contest, even though he
himself benefited but little from such common efforts. Herbaud
admired Sartre boundlessly; "except when he's asleep, Sartre thinks
all the time," he reported (Memoirs, 358). It was not surprising,
therefore, that Simone finally found a mind superior to her own: "It
was the first time in my life that I had felt intellectually inferior to

anyone else. . ." ("que je me sentais intellectuellement dominée par quelqu'un . . ." [*Memoirs*, 364]).

But Sartre's personality was not narrowly confined to things of the mind. His generosity, his huge infectious good humor, revealed to Simone that there were other aspects of life that she ought to explore. In short, "Sartre corresponded exactly to the dream companion I had longed for since I was fifteen: he was the double in whom I found all my burning aspirations raised to the pitch of incandescence. I should always be able to share everything with him. When I left him at the beginning of August, I knew that he would never go out of my life again" (*Memoirs*, 366).

This quiet, firm certainty requires her to tidy up her emotional life, which she sets out to do after Jacques returns from military service in North Africa. During the eighteen months of his absence, he had never once written her; Simone had chanced upon his former girlfriend and had for a time felt uneasy about Jacques' conventional way of dealing with women. She now finds him still attractive but feels sure she can dismiss him from her life without pangs when she finds out that he himself has decided to marry for money. The pathetic story of Jacques' eventual demise is told in sober words; his end has a tragic dimension, and yet there is also a trace of Romantic irony in the depth of his degradation.

Simone is now free to develop along the lines she once had dreamed of; her future, as she sees it in 1929, is uncluttered by old inhibitions and false loyalties. She is ready for a life of action, of intense intellectual pursuit. Moving into the apartment of her recently widowed grandmother, she is ready to sever all the links that subject her to family considerations. At the same time, her freedom is acknowledged by her parents, and a sounder basis for her independence is created.

CHAPTER 2

The Second Volume of Memoirs—
La Force de L'Age

I *Lessons Drawn from the Echo:*
The Experience of Published Memoirs

IN the first volume of her memoirs, Simone de Beauvoir emphatically resolved to "tell everything," a pledge she manifestly fulfilled or, as some critics would have it, overfulfilled. At the outset of the second volume of these memoirs, she feels compelled to warn her readers not to expect her to tell everything:

> I described my childhood and adolescence without any omissions. But though I have, as I hope, managed to recount the story of my life since then without excessive embarrassment or indiscreetness, I cannot treat the years of my maturity in the same detached way—nor do I enjoy a similar freedom when discussing them. I have no intention of filling these pages with spiteful gossip about myself and my friends: I lack the instinct of a scandalmonger. There are many things which I firmly intend to leave in obscurity. (*Prime*, 10)

The questions of what to include and what to leave out being an author's privilege, the main criterion in evaluations should be an aesthetic one. Problems of veracity are always thorny in memoir writing. Where is the author sincere; is there a pose or an embellishment, conscious or unconscious? Simone de Beauvoir's persistent irony helps the reader to determine the degree to which retrospective judgments have an authentic ring, because that irony tends to deflate any inclination to pomposity.

There are, of course, other criteria in the appreciation of journals or memoirs, even though they may be difficult to establish in an incontrovertible manner. The writer no longer is the same as the one who lived through the experiences related to us. Viewed from the vantage point of maturity, childish likes and dislikes often embarrass the honest memorialist; he or she cannot be expected to divorce thoughts at the time of writing from the more or less dim reminiscences that are to be conjured up. It takes an unusual detachment to speak of oneself with any kind of objectivity or even simple distance.

Irony alone would not have helped the writer to maintain throughout the first three volumes of the account of her life a tone of fair appraisal, of psychological insight so rich in projection of passionate feelings among members of the family or in the amazingly accurate description of the intellectual and moral climate of the times. The patriotic frenzy of the First World War is evoked with a few masterful strokes of the pen: the superpatriotic little Simone, conforming fully to the hysteria then prevalent and puzzled by the rare manifestations of compassion for enemy prisoners and of true humanity by men and women in the French provinces, emerges fresh and in full color.

The depiction of the stifling atmosphere in the *pensionnat* and of family life in the south central provinces of France with its heavy stress on domestic virtues of thrift and ingenuity, on the importance of food; the biting references to the widespread bigotry among Catholic bourgeoisie, to the increasingly meaningless and empty ceremonies, but above all, to the frightful, pathetic situation of all young girls who had to marry in blind, total acceptance of the subjection of women to man—therein lies the greatest value of the first volume of the autobiography. Indeed, all her memoirs were to serve in large part to enhance the testimony she gave in her weightiest essays. Simone de Beauvoir everywhere passionately but in carefully documented ways exposes the plight of young middle class women: they remained chattel up to the middle of the twentieth century.

With remarkable sagacity, the memorialist traced her itinerary as a schoolgirl and a student, where books she was fond of, discoveries she made, ideas that struck her, were the major landmarks. Once in a while, inaccuracies occur, some of which are more ironical as the author manifested great enthusiasm for certain studies or disciplines, and many of her errors occur precisely in those fields. Thus, in the first volume, she told of her juvenile leanings toward geography and of her ecstasy, in later years, flying over long-dreamed-of places; this ecstasy goes side by side with carelessness in the beloved geography, as in the passage where she speaks of the "popes of

Mount Atlas" (*Memoirs*, 361).[1] a boner which the translator religiously kept. Fully aware of such occasional slips, the author concludes her preface to the second volume by saying that it is ". . . likely . . . that my memory has betrayed me over various small details. Such minor errors as the reader may observe should certainly not be taken as invalidating the general veracity of this narrative" (*Prime*, 11), a disclaimer that could cover other mistakes as well.

The second volume yields its own harvest of careless gaffes, the most egregious of which may be found in the title of Boris Pilniak's novel, which is given as *La Volga se jette dans la Mer Baltique* (*Prime*, 43), charitably corrected by the translator. Perhaps such mistakes ought to be explained by the author's stated dislike for finicky exactness in any work;[2] they do, of course, never diminish the value of her colorful yet serious writing about her many explorations of the globe, as her inclinations proved to be genuinely constant. Discovered while she was still very young, her love of nature never died, and it is in evoking this lifelong passion that the writer attains poetic heights in a book not consistently well written. It is this same love of nature that is reflected from the opening pages of the second volume in glowing accounts of walks through the countryside with Sartre, who claimed to be "allergic to chlorophyll" (*Prime*, 17); at the same time, the new volume conveys her exhilaration over the newly won independence.

II   A Two Year Lease That Never Became Cancelled

The great event in Simone's life was the perfect understanding between Sartre and herself, a union that was to last to the present through storms big and small, crises due to external circumstances as well as to human factors. Respecting her distaste for marriage, which he actually shared and had expressed even before being close to her, one day that happy summer of 1929 Sartre said: "Let's sign a two year lease . . ." (*Prime*, 17), which was to be the start of their lifelong association. She then felt with keen foresight what became the greatest single certainty in her life: "I knew that no harm could ever come to me from him—unless he were to die before I died" (*Prime*, 17). As she views their long union, she recalls the frame of mind both shared at the time: "one single aim fired us, the urge to embrace all experience, and to bear witness concerning it" (*Prime*, 26).

The quiet certainty of having found her life's companion who shared her goals is all the more wondrous as at first Simone had not felt Sartre's equal at all. She noted that "day after day, and all day long I set myself up against Sartre, and in our discussions I was simply not in his class. . . ."[3] If such was her feeling with regard to Sartre's intellect compared to hers, she nevertheless felt a rugged sort of self-confidence and needed no special comforting from anybody when it came to assessing her own potential. This appears quite clearly from a passage at the start of the fourth part of volume one of the memoirs:

> I would go back to the Library . . . among these specialists, scholars, researchers, and thinkers I felt at home. I no longer felt rejected by my environment; it was I who had rejected it in order to enter that society—of which I saw here a cross section—in which all those minds that are interested in finding out the truth communicate with one another across the distances of space and time. I, too, was taking part in the effort which humanity makes to know, to understand, to express itself. I was engaged in a great collective enterprise which would release me forever from the bonds of loneliness. (*Memoirs*, 301–302)

Her search for identity ended, because she felt at one with the scholarly world, Simone de Beauvoir set out to follow her vocation or what at the time she thought was her vocation. For a time, she lived in Paris, rather frugally, by tutoring and substituting in a girls' *lycée* (where she did not feel like imposing strict discipline on the ten year old, thereby forfeiting renewal of her contract, which did not upset her too much). At the same time, she absorbed knowledge through every pore, every avenue of learning and seeing; she continued to explore the countryside with friends, new and old; she read avidly and went to see movies of all kinds with Sartre, who shared her keen interest in this still new form of art. She was then assigned to the *lycée* in Marseille, which meant she was to be separated by the greatest possible geographic distance from Sartre, who had been appointed to the *lycée* in Le Havre.

Facing that prospect, Sartre proposed marriage, which both had always emphatically condemned as a moribund bourgeois institution. Sartre, "faced with my state of panic, proposed to revise our plans. If we got married, he said, we would have the advantage of a double post, and in the long run such a formality would not seriously affect our way of life" (*Prime*, 65). The prospect took Simone unawares:

Hitherto we had not even considered the possibility of submitting ourselves to the common customs and observances of our society, and in consequence the notion of getting married had simply not crossed our minds. It
offended our principles. There were many points over which we hesitated,
but our anarchism was as deep-dyed and aggressive as that of the old
Libertarians, and stirred us, as it had done them, to withstand any en-
croachment by society on our private affairs. We were against in-
stitutionalism, which seemed incompatible with freedom, and likewise opposed to the bourgeoisie, from whom such a concept stemmed. We found it
normal to behave in accordance with our convictions, and took the unmar-
ried state for granted. Only some very serious consideration would have
made us bow before conventions which we found repellent. (*Prime*, 65–66)

Mere geographic distance in the end was not found by them to be
such a consideration; they felt secure in their attachment to each
other; Simone, for one, also thought of Sartre's freedom, which
would be jeopardized should he sacrifice his independence, if only
on paper. The one conceivable reason for getting married would
have been the presence of children, and here the memorialist restates her fundamental aversion to ever giving birth, for all sorts of
motives, some personal—she disliked small babies; some ideological—she refused the thought of "unjustifiably" increasing the
world's already exploding population. Motherhood, she writes,
"simply was not my natural lot in life, and by remaining childless, I
was fulfilling my proper function" (*Prime*, 67).

One may or may not accept this view and the attitude that went
with it; besides her elaboration of this point in *The Second Sex*, it
becomes evident through repeated statements in the memoirs that
this is one of the basic themes in a life devoted to the intellect.
However, Simone de Beauvoir was to develop a valid theory of the
rights of persons—women, children, old people—for which her
early impulsions and trends in her thinking were to form a basis.
She was to examine some of these problems all her life.

Simone de Beauvoir refused to see her relationship to Sartre only
in terms of children or through bourgeois eyes. She found in him a
disinterested, mature adviser, a friend on whom she could always
rely. For him, she often acted as a whetstone, enabling him to fully
exercise his intellect. He could try on her any experimental thoughts
and projects; she would find in him, in turn, the most incorruptible
mentor. Of course, there is much more to their unique, harmonious
relationship; leaving out the exhilarating joint explorations, the

good-natured banter, the private jokes and allusions unperceived by outsiders, the common bonds grew through shared readings, travels, friendships with others, and almost continuous daily contact, despite the separate living arrangements they always maintained.

Their union breathes so much warmth and deep mutual respect, it comprises such complete reliance of one on the other, that the proud independence kept by them at the same time may surprise; it is an independence both mental and material, if not moral. The intellectual congeniality equals the sentimental attachment, if one can at all apply such unsuitable categories when two persons are so deeply fond of each other, so firmly allied and yet autonomous.

III   Start of a Professional Life

"In the whole of my life I have experienced no special moment that I can label 'decisive'; but certain occasions have become so charged with significance in retrospect that they stand out from my past as clearly as if they had been truly great events. Looking back, I feel that my arrival in Marseille marked a complete new turn in my career" (*Prime*, 75). Standing at the top of the big staircase near the railway station, the young teacher who had just alighted in the Mediterranean metropolis scanned the horizon with a mixture of elation over the vastness of her uncertain future and of anxiety at the countless unknown houses and people she would encounter. She reported for her job and was given some perfunctory help in locating living quarters; getting acquainted with her new colleagues became a harrowing experience, as older members of the teaching profession expected to be treated with deference by their juniors without feeling called on to reciprocate or even to offer the slightest bit of advice. Undaunted by the gruff reception she at first received, the new *agrégée* concentrated on doing her assigned work well enough and sought peace and relaxation in nature, on long walks through the countryside, despite dire warnings from her colleagues who frowned on anyone—especially a woman—setting out alone along the still rather wild trails.

The coolness of the reception, incidentally, was not due to her colleagues' rudeness only; Simone is frank in admitting that she refrained from even the most elementary civility, entering the teachers' conference room without saying hello and bending to other small courtesies. Uncompromising then, she recognizes that

she must have antagonized people all through her life by being curt
and a rigorous nonconformist. Such admissions, however, are only
part of the story. At other times, the memorialist allows us to see
more definitely unpleasant features in her earlier self. Thus she
relates how she set out with her sister, who was visiting her, on one
of her ambitious walks, when Hélène became violently ill. Simone
left her at the hospice with the understanding that they were going
to meet on the homeward bus and continued her excursion alone;
later that night she found her sister seriously ill, and even at that
time she somewhat regretted her callous behavior:

Today I can scarcely imagine how I could have brought myself to leave her
shivering in that gloomy refectory as I did. Generally, it is true, I showed
consideration for other people, and I was very fond of my sister. Sartre often
used to tell me that I was schizophrenic, that instead of adapting my
schemes to reality I pursued them in the teeth of circumstances, regarding
hard facts as something merely peripheral. In Sainte-Baume, in fact, I was
prepared to deny my sister's existence, rather than deviate from my prepared program: she had always fallen in so loyally with all my schemes that I
refused even to envisage the possibility of her disrupting them on this
occasion. What Sartre called schizophrenic seemed to me an extreme and
aberrant form of my particular brand of optimism. I refused, as I had done
when I was twenty, to admit that life contained any wills apart from my
own. (*Prime*, 78)

Teaching did not demand too much of an effort; every spare moment was devoted to outdoor life; a simple pastime became an
all-devouring passion. ("I managed to turn a pastime into a most
exacting duty . . . " [*Prime*, 76–77]), indeed the central preoccupation during her time in Marseille. Simone even rejected conventional gear for this unconventional endeavor, and instead of attiring
herself in nailed boots and "respectable" loden, her rope-soled *es-
padrilles* became the trademark of her expeditions. No wonder her
colleagues shuddered and snickered at such utter amateurism.

Despite warnings from just about everyone experienced in hiking, Simone ventured on mountain paths by herself, savoring her
freedom and the rough beauty of the unspoiled southern country,
forgetting some elementary precautions, so that she had more than
one near brush with accident or even death. Her life became
sharply divided between the official side, her teaching, and her very
own domain, the exploration of the world and its people.

She was not exactly aided in her adjustment, to a degree, to Marseille society by the ambiguous reception reserved to her by a married woman colleague who at first timidly invited her into her home only to confide in Simone the unfortunate passion she conceived for her. Naive to the point of ignorance, the young teacher nevertheless managed to placate the unhappy woman through appeals to her reason and respectability, but the episode, while making her more cautious in her dealings with individuals, failed to dampen her enthusiasm at the discovery of nature and of people. True, she had earlier remarked how uniquely equipped she found herself to make the best of anything: "I have never met anyone, in the whole of my life, who was so well equipped for happiness as I was, or who labored so stubbornly to achieve it. No sooner had I caught a glimpse of it than I concentrated upon nothing else. If I had been promised renown and glory at the price of happiness, I should have refused. . ." (*Prime*, 28).

Never one to put her light under a bushel, especially not on intellectual matters, Simone de Beauvoir excels in painting her own portrait, warts and all, to an extent that she sometimes appears in distinctly unfavorable light: after all, such traits are referring to a distant past. Thus, she recalls, "I was an impetuous creature, with more passion than subtlety in my make-up. My trouble was an excess of good nature: I drove so straight for my goal that on occasion I showed myself lacking in tact. . ." (35).

As to the dangers faced in her adventurous walks through the mountains of Provence, she manifested a curious blend of fatalistic blind trust in nature and of an extreme self-reliance that must sometimes appear juvenile: "and in any case, there were certain things such as accidents, severe illness, or rape, which simply *could not happen* to me" (79–80; the emphasis is the translator's). Many more illustrations of this attitude appear in the memoirs, positively and negatively, as for instance the shock at discovering that it could happen to her, first during a dangerous accidental slide on rocks, and subsequently when she had pneumonia (233).

IV *Character Asperities*

This same disposition is reflected all through the different volumes of her memoirs; sometimes it takes on a melancholy sort of self-irony, as in the case of sentimental disappointments. The same trend is shown by the novelist in various situations in novels and stories. It is perhaps the most consistently recurring leitmotiv, indicating the author's fundamental attitude toward herself. In retrospect, she applies incisive irony and delivers an intentionally dispassionate recital of her life, her character, her nature.

Flattery of any kind, whether of herself or others, is totally alien to Simone de Beauvoir, a virtue which occasionally may upset those unused to her ways but which makes her rare compliments all the more valuable. Given to enthusiasm for the beauties of nature, the writer never spares her criticism: her uncompromising integrity is never at fault, no matter how advantageous it might be to remain silent. This trait may explain why certain appraisals of her work by critics have an acerbic, aggressive tone, unwarranted by the thrust of what she wrote or said in public, although she did take sides resolutely, be it in politics (ever since the Algerian War), in social matters, or on the question of women's liberation. No doubt it is the very sincerity with which she wrote her memoirs that contributed to the antagonism. Simone de Beauvoir is far from diplomatic and does not feel the need to mend her fences, which infuriates many who voice censorious blame over this or that element in her writings for moral or aesthetic reasons far more than for any philosophic ones.

Sincerity, incidentally, is an inadequate term when one tries to define the kind of human message the memorialist conveys in her often rude approach, implicating others, to be sure, in situations that are sometimes unpleasant, but never sparing herself either. The immediacy with which the memoirs reveal facts and traits is disarming, because Simone de Beauvoir is not aiming at artistic effects as much as at reconstructing the past. She has scrutinized her younger self thoroughly before sharing the conclusions with her readers, as in this passage of quiet matter of fact statement: "Perhaps it is hard for anyone to learn the art of peaceful coexistence with somebody else: certainly I had never been capable of it. Either I reigned supreme or sank into the abyss" (54)—a finding possibly unnecessary in the flow of reminiscences but refreshingly honest from one who had to overcome the temptation of intellectual arrogance.

Likewise, we would never have known but for the author's unhesitating record of her qualms and pangs what she went through by having to see Sartre under conditions of strain and stress during his military service when they were able to meet only for brief moments in the afternoon, unable to spend nights together. So strong was her sense of loss, of need, that she comments on the unnatural separation at some length, very openly, voicing her distress: "the notion that I partook of a condition common to all mankind gave me no consolation at all. It wounded my pride to find myself condemned to a subordinate rather than a commanding role where the private movements of my blood were concerned . . ." (56).

Such frank avowals are rare in the annals of autobiography, and the writer at this stage disclaims any militancy in the feminist ranks, as she wanted to function as an individual only, giving us a fine and sensitive portrayal of sexual drive, of irrepressible desires, and of the difficulty of accepting "contingent" solutions. The former puritan finds herself understanding the "torture suffered by all separated lovers, all couples confronted by the difficulties of finding privacy" (56). These are pages to be pondered by the all too many thoughtless, unfair critics who accuse Simone de Beauvoir of pandering to licentiousness and debauchery because they seem unable to understand the clear beauty of such a human document.

Indeed, it is a most courageous, straight discussion of fundamental human needs, which until then had either been bypassed by writers or exploited for sensationalist, salacious treatment while scientific analysis had not yet tackled the problem at the time that the memoirs were written except in a merely statistical way. Recounting the suffering, the frustrations, the exasperation of physical need, Simone de Beauvoir achieved one of the most difficult victories, which she couches in simple, moving terms, a victory over the self, regaining control and mindful of all her obligations, through a firm analysis of the situation in a calm, rational account that offers a clear picture of the dilemma typical for millions of young people in a world ruled by tradition and taboos.

Just as she was blunt in the statement of elemental needs, she remained perspicacious when it came to evaluating her own writing talent over the years. Time and time again she rewrote her novel, finding some of the earlier chapters quite good but realizing that she lacked the skill to tie in lived experience, though she did use the lives of friends and acquaintances to inject authenticity into her characters. She thus was not swayed by the praise that Sartre and other friends cautiously dispensed on portions of what she had

written and in her memoirs dispassionately summarizes the plots of the various versions, pinpointing their respective strengths and weaknesses without any sentimentality.

V A Taste for the Dingy

Enthusiastic in her love of nature, thirsting for sights, for as yet undiscovered mountain tops, for the freshness and whiteness of ski trails, for monuments and paintings, Simone de Beauvoir at all times was receptive to beauty. She humorously tells how frequently Sartre disagreed with her when it became a matter of additional fatigue and risk to climb up yet another steep and stony hillside in search of ancient ruins, when she would leave on a lonely trail and conquer all by herself a bare rock wall to admire faint relics of a bygone civilization.

Her quest for beauty is a lifelong addiction, and the description of cities, mountain ranges, beaches, evokes nature in often moving words. She never gives a mere travelogue, a guidebook description of indifferent, impersonal findings, but, as in Greece, she abstracts from her own vision and recreates an impression of personal relationship to the country visited, "not concerned . . . to draw a picture of Greece, but simply of the life we led there" (244).

In so doing, however, she succeeded in giving an extraordinarily rich and colorful picture, one that included in the very Baudelairian sense the sounds and smells along with the colors, not to mention flavors. The primacy of sight had been demonstrated by the author early in her memoirs ("of the five senses there was one that I valued far above the rest: sight . . ." [70]), but that preference does not prevent the writer from suggesting with strong realism a number of perceptual notations in a highly effective way.

That beauty was her first object of search appears from every page of travelogue she wrote all through her life, and her evocation of beauty is practically always infectious and stimulating. Yet she did not forget human misery in visiting the many different countries and continents she saw and hardly ever closed her mind to social problems. Indeed, these affected her very early in life and were to increasingly preoccupy and puzzle her, to the point where she made hers the most urgent claims for justice and reform, as in the case of workers having to spend their days in unhealthy conditions. These struck her for the first time while on a visit through her cousin's Lyon electric socket factory (51).

Again, in Greece, during the Metaxas dictatorship, when children threw stones at the French tourists, there is the stirring of conscience; in this circumstance, however, Sartre, Bost, and Simone still affected to think they were not the intended targets, and "through thoughtlessness and self-deception we managed to defend ourselves against any harsh realities that might have spoiled our holidays" (242). Thus there is not necessarily a consistent line of social concern at the time of the experience, but the truthful notation of past callousness indicates a thorough change in attitude.

The clinical detachment with which Simone de Beauvoir noted how she acted during her trips comes close to cynicism; yet anyone reading the record of her constant preoccupation with social themes throughout her work cannot for one moment mistake the candor for anything but a positive mark of deeply human commitment. But it is possibly the professed distaste for "humanism," cruelly mocked by Sartre—a distaste shared by both—that made them insensitive to actual suffering in individuals, at least as far as the literary rendering of such feelings is concerned.

For there is no dearth in Simone de Beauvoir's narrative of her travels with regard to sensitivity to social conditions: everywhere she is quick to see the prevailing facts—incredible misery and squalor in Naples, side by side with the splendor of colors and the ironically huge wealth in food display; the poverty of Greek peasants, and the oppressive character of the Metaxas regime; and later, on her trip to Brazil, as already on her postwar foray into Portugal, she always sees the negative side together with the bright one. Her eyes were open to beauty, but she is fully able to spot blemishes, and she never recoils from her responsibility in giving the full picture of a country, including slums. In viewing the hovels of the desperately poor, Beauvoir makes it clear that she condemns the system that allows such disgraceful discrepancies between the rich and those deprived of even the bare essentials.

If beauty is what her heart is set on when she is traveling, a curious inclination drives her to places of quaint if not shabby decor whenever she has the choice between a clean, modern cafe and a dingy one where the upholstery is ripped open, the floor littered, the table cloth stained, as in the Brasserie Paul in Rouen, long her favorite spot. In modern art, her tastes usually go to the nonobjective and against any academic or realist painting; she appreciated Salvador Dali's "liquefying watches" (152), and felt a "kind of delighted horror" at seeing the then elegant beaches of Trouville and Deauville (155).

This reaction of a refined mind, open to the sleazy charm of rundown old taverns, closed to clean, well-lighted cafes, finds its expression time after time, for example, at the Brasserie Chandivert in Caen: "I found its provincial jollity most depressing . . ." (154). It is almost a foregone conclusion that any "normal," clear-cut site is to be spurned, while gloomy, musty, dusty, seedy places, if possible with broken down furniture and torn upholstery, are appealing.

Such taste for the shady side of surfaces cannot exist without corresponding opinions and concepts:

> We united in hating Sunday crowds, fashionable ladies and gentlemen, the provinces, family life, children, and any sort of "humanism," records the author speaking of the accord felt between Sartre and her with their young friend, Olga. "We liked exotic music; the *quais* along the Seine, with their coal barges and dockside loafers; low, disreputable little bars; and the silent loneliness of the night." (204)

The deep-set dislike for, and distrust of, "humanism" echoes Sartre's known disdain for softness in materials, for sweet tastes, for everything other than the hard surfaces like the famous pebble, an inclination shared by his companion ever since she was a child. While claiming "I was not a priori set on playing the Bohemian" (233), Simone de Beauvoir, on being appointed to the *Lycée Molière* in Paris, again chose a hotel room rather than an apartment—too much bother looking for one, she states. At that very time, the couple selects as their headquarters a neighborhood cafe "which we found enchanting. There was a downstairs room which, with its imitation leather banquettes, marble-top tables, and lighting reminded us of the Brasserie Paul; the walls were covered with dark fretted paneling, for all the world like a Neapolitan hearse . . ." (233).

Many of the settings in her own novels remind us of such favorite places, especially in *She Came to Stay*, but also in some of the later works of fiction. It is perhaps owing to this tendency toward the odd, the decidedly antibourgeois, that, nearing thirty years of age, she was to seek the thrill—if not the danger, since she was always sure to be able to defend herself against too persistent dancers—in the bars of Rue de Lappe in Paris and, later on, more as a spectator only, Rue Blomet, where blacks danced with whites, and in all the many shady amusement places in Rouen and Le Havre. As she put it in her memoirs, at the time of leaving Rouen: "It was high time that both Marco [a friend, also a model for one of Sartre's novelistic heroes] and I left Rouen: our reputations were beginning to suffer in no uncertain fashion . . ." (210).

But, of course, nothing particularly shocking had happened during her years in the provinces, and the tall tales whispered on her account lack any serious foundation. Mostly, the fact that she had treated her students like adults and talked to them as responsible persons capable of making certain judgments was held against her. Whenever she had insisted, in class, on reading books classified as objectionable, storms of protest had originated in groups of indignant parents; most of these storms had died down when the *Lycée* administrators showed good sense and stopped the matter then and there after advising Simone of the nature of the complaint. Sanctions were not to be used against her, yet enough small-minded envy existed to provide grist for the gossip mills.

VI *Milestones in the Making of a Writer*

The second volume of memoirs encompasses a long, eventful stretch of life and of contemporary history, from the time Beauvoir launched on a teaching career, in 1929, until her final breakthrough as a novelist, and the liberation of France, in 1944. Written with the obvious goal of baring her evolution, often intertwined with Sartre's, the book also offers probing analyses of political, intellectual, and social changes over the fifteen year span; she shows capsule views of some of her friends, miniature portraits of people both famous and obscure, and incidents hilarious as well as tragic in the lives of people she knew.

In the course of the narrative, the author brushes a lively fresco of life in the provinces as she experienced it during her early career as a philosophy teacher, first in Marseille, then in Rouen. What is remarkable, from the start, is the voracity with which she reads essential books on all sorts of subjects; views films and plays; listens to music, one of her lifelong joys; meets people whom she describes with uncommonly colorful characteristic detail.

Among the friends she and Sartre made, sometimes separately, often together, are a number of former students of either, whose lives occasionally accompany those of the two writers, be it in harmony or in conflict or, as in the cases of Olga and Lise*, alternately in harmony and in clashes. Trips taken with several of these friends turned out to be more gratifying, even though here, too, notes of discord are recorded, as on the Spanish automobile trip with Madame Lemaire and Pagniez when a few moments of irritation occurred, as Beauvoir notes with her typical lack of inhibition, over Sartre's and her innocent but oblivious self-centeredness, leaving all the transportation problems and chores to Pagniez. The events noted by her on such trips gain a particular relief, unheard of in smooth travelogues where everything always works out perfectly. On practically all of her many trips, the memorialist notes at least some minor hitches; these never interfere with the enjoyment and often actually enhance the sense of adventure.

The volume also gives substantial space to a discussion of the various stages of her novelistic writing and to the growth of other ideas which she would elaborate in essay form or use for her play. Yielding on details and methods but firm in her consistent search for the right expression of her thoughts, Simone de Beauvoir listened to suggestions from Sartre and other friends who by and large encouraged her to persist, even when the novel at first was rejected by publishers.

The most valuable function this second volume of memoirs fulfills is probably the vivid evocation of the atmosphere of the thirties. It shows the long delusion of left-wing intellectuals that they could live on as before, paying little heed to the growing storm signs on the political horizon. Stressing mostly events that were to prove fateful in retrospect, Simone de Beauvoir shows herself fully sharing in the naive optimism most Europeans demonstrated in those days. As the situation grew increasingly more threatening, she had been reluctant to join in the pessimistic evaluation that Sartre and a few farsighted people made, especially after the outbreak of the Spanish Civil War. Hoping against hope, Simone was clinging to a way of life that was possible only in a world unaffected by totalitarianism and wars, where the individual would remain free to choose, to glean the pleasures of existence, to learn and work in unison with others and become useful to mankind.

VII   *Apolitical Attitudes*

The one overwhelming impression that more and more transpires in the pages of her memoirs is her perfect openness in recounting every aspect of her life, for example in stating how little both she and Sartre were interested in politics in the late twenties and early thirties: "public affairs bored us"; and again: "At every level we failed to face the weight of reality, priding ourselves on what we called our 'radical freedom' " (18). To this undisguised admission she adds: "As our ignorance kept us unaware of most of the problems that might have worried us, we remained quite content with these revisions of doctrine, and indeed thought ourselves very daring" (19).

A closer look at the author's evolution from a completely nonpolitical mind to one involved in action is necessary if we want to understand the way in which both writers saw the world and themselves at different stages in their lives. Social concern was expressed early enough by the dutiful daughter of a middle class Catholic family, but despite certain leanings, certain revulsions, she had not felt an urgent need to take sides.

In 1929, a year of profound changes in her life owing to her partial economic emancipation, to the conclusion of her formal education, and to her meeting with Sartre, both these recent *agrégés* felt untouched by either Marxism or psychoanalysis (23). In 1932, the various political events left the couple unaffected mentally, and though vaguely sympathizing with the Communists, "Sartre had not gone to the polls, and nothing could shake us out of our apolitical attitude . . ." (93).

These sympathies for Communism were rather theoretical; a sense of independence prevailed whenever Sartre and Simone felt dutybound to do more than merely sympathize with "the struggle being fought by the working classes: ought we not to join in it?" (111). Despite the recurrent temptation to do so, both intellectuals decided: "that if you belonged to the proletariat you had to be a Communist, but that though the proletarian struggle was of importance to us, it was even so not *our* struggle . . . . We had our own tasks to fulfill, and they were not compatible with joining the party" (111). Both were perfectly lucid as to the indecision that such an attitude reflects and jokingly referred to themselves as "Two *petits-bourgeois* invoking their unwritten work as an excuse for avoiding political commitment . . ." (114).

Some of the perplexities that confronted them then (which, by the way, have never completely subsided, because of the curious alignment of ideological groupings then and now) showed that they were paradoxically attracted by America, whose regime they condemned,

while the USSR that they wholeheartedly admired left them "quite
cold"; "we still were not actively *for* anything" (116). Even when the
Fascist riots of February 6, 1934, broke out, Simone reports that she
followed the events from a distance, "being convinced that it was no
concern of mine" (128), but she adds in retrospect: "I must have
been extremely stubborn to maintain this attitude of indifference . . ." (128). A few days later, when after the Fascist provoca-
tion a huge counterdemonstration was organized by the left, in
which all her friends participated, it never occurred to her to join
them, explaining her abstention by stating that she "was such a
stranger to all practical political activities . . ." (132).

Reminiscing on that same year, 1934, she finds her way of reading
the papers "decidedly frivolous," as she "avoided all problems posed
by Hitler's political activities, and regarded the rest of the world
with an indifferent eye . . ." (172). When one knows how deeply,
ever since the Algerian War, the memorialist has committed herself
to the righting of wrongs, it is indeed striking to note her evolution
over the years from perfect indifference to commitment and actual
militancy.

A small but significant change takes place over the next few
months owing in part to a growing sense of futility, of frustration in
both Sartre and Beauvoir; true, Sartre has still not voted in the 1936
election, which resulted in the triumph of the Popular Front.
Simone de Beauvoir attempts an analysis of the postelectoral sobering in the midst of elated overstatements of political efficiency by
some intellectuals:

> What a lot of pointless fuss! Would it all have seemed so ridiculous to us,
> if we had been given a chance of participating in it? I just don't know. On
> the other hand I am almost certain that if we had found ourselves in a
> position to take effective action we would have done so: our habit of absten-
> tion was largely due to our powerlessness, and we did not a priori object to
> participating in events. The proof of this is that when the strikes came and
> they went through the streets taking up collections for the strikers, we gave
> all we could. . . . (212)

—a point which does not sound very convincing in a society where
others did go out of their way to fight for workers' rights.

In 1938, after being appointed in Paris, to her great satisfaction,
she "passed through one of the most depressing periods of [my]

whole life. I refused to admit that war was even possible, let alone imminent. But it was no use playing the ostrich; the growing perils all around crushed me beneath their weight . . ." (254). An ostrich no longer, Simone just the same kept on considering her private domain inviolate; political realities were to be held at arm's length as long as possible, through the process that Sartre and she had baptized "schizophrenia": whenever possible, consider only the immediate fulfillment of a desire, regardless of the outside world. Thus for instance, at the time of the Munich crisis, she was loath to change her plans for hiking through the mountains, and when Sartre encouraged her that summer to go, "My divided mind [ma schizophrénie] easily triumphed over my disquiet, and I let him catch the train without me" (267). Other examples of the same disposition abound. It would be difficult to find other memorialists in our time capable of painting portraits so bluntly truthful.

When the Munich agreement was announced, she was "delighted and felt not the slightest pang of conscience at [my] reaction. I felt I had escaped death, now and forever. There was even an element of triumph in my relief. Decidedly, I thought, I was born lucky: no misfortune would ever touch me" (268). One should note that in this instance, both of these leading themes overlap, the personal feeling of privilege, born lucky, crowning the relief over the crisis past, without any commitment to snap out of her apolitical attitude for good. As we have seen with regard to the feeling of safety from misfortunes, that was at times badly shattered.

No apologies are needed, in the author's eyes, over her long inertia in matters that must have appeared increasingly urgent and vital to her friends, to all those around her in the thirties. There is some irony in the fact that for her, as for millions of people all over the world, events shaped a thorough change in her outlook; once the feeling of privilege was shaken and things could happen to her, too, the basis of her aloofness was shattered, and action became necessary. It is to her credit that she never concealed her own hesitations.

Neither is any undue leniency used by her in establishing how very long both Sartre and she remained politically indifferent. For years, what interested both of them was the advancement of social justice, to be sure, but not the day by day occurrences or even the great outlines of world politics. They focused almost exclusively on crime chronicles, which to them were baring social evils at the root of most misdeeds. It was not until the left-wing parties in France started to unite in the Popular Front, in 1934, that the thrill of action moved them for the first time, and from then on they followed the political developments with a measure of attention. The outbreak of the Spanish Civil War, in 1936, could not fail to sharpen that interest. It had an impact on the majority of young Frenchmen of the left. From that time on, Simone de Beauvoir and Sartre knew their own lives depended on the outcome of what happened in Spain: "The Spanish Civil War for the next two and a half years was to dominate our lives . . ." (220).

Yet, even that late awakening to political reality did not go without some reticence due no doubt to the long aversion to things other than purely intellectual. In 1935, Beauvoir notes, "both Sartre and I had its victory [The Popular Front's] very much at heart; and yet our individualism hampered our more progressive instincts, and we still maintained the attitude which had restricted us to the role of witnesses . . ." (211). During the tightening crisis of the Spanish Civil War, when nonintervention so obviously undermined the strength of the republic, the paralyzing helplessness of their situation struck Sartre and his companion:

For the first time in our lives, because the fate of Spain concerned us so deeply, indignation *per se* was no longer a sufficient outlet for us: our political impotence, far from furnishing us with an alibi, left us feeling hopeless and desolate. And it was so absolute: we were mere isolated nobodies. Nothing we could say or do in favor of intervention would carry the slightest weight. (231)

Much of the later deep commitment of both writers must be understood in light of that early feeling of impotence (212).[4] After they both had become famous, in the fifties, they felt obligated to show the way, and during the difficult years of the struggle for Algerian independence, for an end to the American war in Vietnam, for many causes involving rights of men, they unceasingly and unsparingly went to the defense of the oppressed.

It was not until 1940, during the "phony war" when he came to Paris for a brief furlough, that Sartre made a decided break with his apolitical past:

He had firmly made up his mind to hold aloof from politics no longer. His new morality . . . required every man to shoulder the responsibility of his situation in life; and the only way in which he could do so was to transcend that situation by engaging upon some course of action. Any other attitude was mere escapist pretense, a masquerade based upon insincerity. It will be clear that a radical change had taken place in him—and in me too, since I rallied to his point of view immediately; for not so long ago our first concern had been to keep our situation in life at arm's length by means of fantasy, deception, and plain lies. . . . (342)

Since she made a clean breast of past failures, it is essential to reassess the many expressions of seeming indifference in political matters that Simone de Beauvoir entered in her memoirs over the years and to put them in perspective. There is first a moment, right after a severe bout with pneumonia, in 1937, when the convalescent felt powerless to fight against the evils of the world; she "asked nothing better than to forget them . . ." (235). And then there are the many days during the German Occupation when she recorded in what seemed a rather frivolous manner unexpected succulent menus in time of general dearth, while appearing less attentive to the gradual disappearance of many of her friends or associates, Jews or *résistants*. What may strike the reader as the wrong kind of priorities will be explained in a subsequent section of this chapter; suffice it to say now that Simone de Beauvoir displays relentless eagerness to "testify," even if it had to be against herself, and to illustrate human frailties through her own example.

VIII   *Adjusting to the War*

The Second World War broke out over the German invasion of Poland, September 1, 1939. While the German Army and Air Force crushed the Poles' heroic resistance, made hopeless when the Soviet Union also intervened, invading Eastern Poland, the Western front remained practically stable and quiet from September 1939 through May 1940. The unprovoked German attacks against Denmark and Norway in April 1940, followed by the violation of Dutch, Belgian, and Luxembourg neutrality, signaled the start of the Battle of France, after May 10, 1940. In a few weeks, German armies had broken through the French defenses, and on June 14 they took Paris.

The ensuing armistice gave Germany control over roughly two thirds of France; the Germans also annexed Alsace-Lorraine. They made German military occupation a reality first in the "occupied zone" of France, and after the Allied landings in North Africa, in

November 1942, in the whole of France. After an initial period of shocked passivity, when they were too stunned to think of continuing the war, many Frenchmen began to detach themselves from the weak and corrupt Fascist regime in Vichy.

Whereas only a minority of Frenchmen actively participated in the Resistance against the Nazis, the vast majority of Frenchmen sympathized with the victims of Nazi persecution: Jews, Freemasons, Communists, pacifists, Socialists, many Catholics, were herded into prisons and concentration camps by the German military and their dreaded secret police, the Gestapo. Thousands of Frenchmen were indeed arrested, some of whom had participated in acts of sabotage against German military installations. But many were merely suspected of "delicts of opinion" or just arbitrarily held under arrest.

Besides the French victims of the Nazis, uncounted masses of foreigners living in France were hounded: Polish miners, Italian anti-Fascists, German political refugees, Spanish Republicans (of which there were over a million and a half in France), and, of course, tens of thousands of Jews, mostly foreign born; but as the war went on, French Jews, too, were surrendered by the Vichy regime to the German camps. Most of them never returned: the death camps saw few survivors.

It was the general fear of being arrested and tortured—a fear far deeper than that of death itself—that prevailed in those years. Moreover, the Germans' evergrowing need for manpower to replace their soldiers who had begun to die by the hundreds of thousands in Africa and in Soviet Russia was felt all over Europe where forced labor became an institution. Compulsory labor service, initially heralded as a great "European" gesture of support and solidarity with the "Champion" in the fight against Communism, sought to send all able-bodied Europeans into German factories and farms.

As soon as compulsory labor started, the immense majority of young Frenchmen went underground in order to escape deportation to Germany—for that is what the labor service amounted to. Thus, a mass of Frenchmen became set against the Germans, a factor which ultimately helped defeat the Nazis, when French Resistance in cooperation with the Allied armies fought the German occupation and eventually succeeded in expelling the German armies from French soil.

Concurrently with the constant fear of arrest and deportation to an all too certain fate went the problem of food supply. Every item of essential need was rationed. Without ration cards, an individual was doomed to die of starvation. It took nationwide complicity to provide the hundreds of thousands of fugitive Frenchmen with forged ration and identity cards, enabling them to survive.

Small wonder if all through the war, particularly during the Occupation, everybody in French talked about food constantly; it had become an obsession, but also a vital necessity, and people developed all sorts of skills hitherto unused to be able to exist. Furthermore, Sartre and Simone had had the alarming experience of coming very near actual starvation during their trip to the Pyrenees, in the summer of 1942, when Sartre collapsed from inanition after they reached the safe haven of Madame Lemaire's house in La Pouèze, not far from Angers.

As has been shown, both Sartre and Beauvoir had lived with growing awareness of the danger of war, though Sartre proved to be pessimistic about the chance of keeping the peace, while his companion chose to minimize the threatening reality and to enjoy life as best she could. When the catastrophe became inevitable, and Sartre along with millions of others was mobilized, Simone bravely adjusted to the new conditions, working eagerly but also continuing to see movies, to go skiing—the small pleasures left her in her isolation.

Her wartime diary, kept intermittently, in its down to earth seriousness sounds like the report of a honeybee, flying from flower to flower, busy and determined, gathering the sweetness left in life. Sober to the point of complete detachment, she tells of her highly illegal visit with Sartre in the war zone in Alsace in tones so impersonal and laconic one would think she went to see her grandfather and not her lover.

The ups and downs of morale during the phony war appear with great clarity; they never hamper her intellectual activity, and a constant growth is evident in her mind even in those difficult months. When the events of war and defeat accelerate with staggering violence, Simone shows herself just as panicky as everybody else, and her exodus parallels those of countless Frenchmen on the roads and the overflowing trains. It may appear strange, in this context, that she never once mentions her parents—not until she returns to Paris after the start of the Occupation and meets her father by sheer coincidence on the terrace of a cafe.

Incidents during the exodus are recalled with plastic exactness, and the behavior of people under the extraordinary stress of flight, bombardment, loss of property, but above all loss of hope, of contact with loved ones, is movingly but also sharply sketched. One can practically smell the air full of smoke from the burning reservoirs or ammunition dumps; hear the buzzing of rumors everywhere in the collapsing French army; sense the enormity of the confusion through which a whole civilized country shrank into a pathetic heap of fearful, blindly groping masses in search only of the most immediately needed goods. The first contacts, at a distance, with the German military are cautious and, in spite of a degree of curiosity, reserved. Circumspection is Simone's main attribute over the next few months, although she remains as adventurous as ever in her undaunted drive to get back to Paris at any price. Sheer vitality and energy hoisted her onto the automobile that through endless futile waiting hours in search of fuel got Simone to the waystation, whence an unexpected bit of luck afforded her the chance to be driven back to Paris smoothly enough.

She minutely, often humorously, describes how life in Paris, from most precarious conditions, became tolerable; how she managed to resume contact with friends; how she found employment at once, as philosophy teachers had become scarce. The latter part of 1940 is filled with anxiety, first over Sartre's whereabouts—he was a prisoner of war, as a million and a half Frenchmen were then—next over his chances to be released or to escape; finally over the problem of how to feed her friends.

With boundless energy and admirable resourcefulness, she went about her task of supplying whatever was available and of organizing meals for her circle of friends. The idea of this reputed bluestocking cooking meals that found approval, in a hotel room, on make-shift ranges is not without its spice. But Simone accomplishes this chore with the same drive that animates her throughout her life, finding satisfaction in marshaling the meager provisions she was able to get; defending her hard-won supplies against mice and worms; saving as much as possible of the half-rotten content of food parcels that her friend Madame Lemaire sent her by freight; and going to extreme lengths to make such rescued foods palatable.

More serious problems arose over the political situation. Sartre had attempted the creation of a resistance network, "Socialisme et Liberté"; he was to find out after a few months that intellectuals lacked the experience of clandestine political fight, at least in wartime France. Faced with the growing danger of risking the arrest of his associates in this endeavor, he regretfully gave up his plan, devoting his energies to resistance as a writer. In moving words, Simone traces the fate of a few of those brave men she had encountered during the planning stage of Sartre's abortive attempt, who paid with their lives their participation in active resistance groups that were raided and dismantled.

She also recounts the fate of some of the regular customers of her favorite cafe during the war years and after, Le Flore, a meeting place for young people from all over Europe. Having grown attached to a few of these, her sense of loss is keen when one after the other disappears. Most of them were taken to camps never to return; a few, like the charming nineteen year old Bourla, were shot. The cafe, of course, always a place where Frenchmen spend a large portion of their lives, had become a real necessity for Beauvoir because, owing to fuel shortages and rationing, it was simply too cold in her hotel room for her to work. Her daily routine could not be reconstructed without the cafe atmosphere, where she felt comfortable, warm, and removed from many of the woes of the Occupation.

IX   *Oases in the Middle of War*

Sartre had had his first novel, *Nausea*, published in 1938; his philosophical treatises were being published during the war, and he had become acquainted with a number of literary figures. Through such associations and chance meetings, their circle of friends eventually grew, comprising Leiris, Queneau, Camus, and later on, Genet, but also Giacometti, Picasso, and their old friend Dullin. As a reaction against the depressing monotony of days during the war, shortened by the curfew, fiestas were organized in a succession of apartments where the group served real banquets conjured up through careful hoarding of hard to get foods and spirits, usually launched by some dramatic performance or the reading of poetry.

By necessity, these parties lasted all night and left an impression of joyful communion despite the nearness of danger and the closeness of death and destruction. There is a very strange charm in the description of these feasts that might appear shocking to some. In her book, Geneviève Gennari has emphasized the importance of "fetes or parties" in Simone de Beauvoir's work, but here we receive a firsthand report that is laced with lyrical detail about the kind of fraternal inebriation that occurred during a fiesta—and all this while the Nazis kept arresting people and the war went on.

The note of frivolous unawareness of the presence of war is sounded more than once; skiing during the last winter before the Liberation, Simone notes: "I enjoyed myself considerably, and ate well," which is perfectly normal if one remembers that human beings are able to concentrate on negative aspects of life only to a certain extent and need relief in any form. After all, soldiers at the front are given shows and other entertainment to take their minds off the tragedy of everyday routine. In Beauvoir's case, she writes what may be the simplest rationale behind the frenzy of festivities: "we were all sufficiently inured to anxiety for it not to spoil our capacity for enjoyment altogether" (449).

Yet another expression of this need for the dance on the volcano reads:

I smiled at people, and they smiled back at me. I was pleased with myself, and with them too: my vanity gave itself an enjoyable airing, and the atmosphere of amiability went straight to my head. All these polite remarks and effusive greetings and pleasantries and small talk had some special quality that saved them from being the usual insipid commonplaces; they left a sharp yet unacknowledged aftertaste. A year before we would never have dreamed of gathering together like this and having a noisy, frivolous party that went on for hours. Prematurely, and despite all the threats that still hung over so many of us, we were celebrating victory. (450)

On the whole, Simone de Beauvoir is unapologetic about these bachanalia, considering them as an antidote to the daily confrontation with danger. Her analysis of the function of the fetes converges with Roger Caillois' formula (in *Le Mythe de la Fête*) and Georges Bataille's (*in La Part du Diable*), as she asserts that "every fete has a quality of pathos about it . . . ," adding:

Nocturnal fetes. . . . Beneath the lively wine-flown raptures there is always a faint taste of death, but for one resplendent moment death is reduced to nothingness. Dangers still threatened us; after the hour of our deliverance there would still be disillusions aplenty in store for us. . . . We did not deceive ourselves about this. We merely wanted to snatch a few nuggets of sheer joy from this confusion and intoxicate ourselves with their brightness, in defiance of the disenchantment that lay ahead. (445)

This may be an ex post facto analysis, hardly accurate in every respect for the behavior during the times of duress; but no matter what lay at its basis, the urge to forget was infectious, and there was little choice in the methods at the time. Psychologically, the evocation is cogent; anyone who lived through the war years in Europe has recollections of this kind. It was natural, therefore, that the writer should incorporate such fetes in *The Mandarins*; her fictional feasts match the autobiographical ones, recapturing the ambience felicitously.

Yet, anguish is never far away, and every time Sartre goes to a clandestine meeting of the writers' union, until his safe return his companion is counting the minutes. It is because she measured the torment of all who were separated—having suffered herself during Sartre's war service and captivity—and the far more trying uncertainties of those left behind after arrests, that the memorialist is much more compassionate than she used to be.

Sparing in her use of words to express what she felt after the disappearance of friends, she allows us to see just enough of her very real sympathy for the victims, just enough heartbreak over the absurd and cruel fate of so many promising existences cut short by firing squads and deportation trains. If she may have appeared hard-hearted at the outset, being insecure and inexperienced, she reached emotional maturity together with intellectual acuity as the misery and injustice lasted, as the long-hoped-for Liberation was still not coming.

Much of these variegated experiences went into her writing, naturally, and the erstwhile dilettante learned how to incorporate actual observations into her books. *L'Invitée (She Came to Stay)*, after many rewritings, had been accepted for publication by Gallimard, and the author greeted this piece of good news with "more relief than joy." She was also working on her second novel, *Le Sang des autres (The Blood of Others)*: Camus read the typescript and liked it so much—he called it "a fraternal book" (445)—that he asked the author to permit its publication in the clandestine series of the *Editions de Minuit*, founded by Vercors. Eventually, Liberation came before the book was printed in that series. Jean Grenier commissioned her to write a philosophic essay which she wrote alongside her play, *Les Bouches inutiles*. She notes, toward the end of the second volume of memoirs, that from that time on she "always had something to say" and that "each book henceforth impelled me toward its successor" (479).

The major reason for this newly won certainty about her literary vocation is the increasing preoccupation with death. Ever since her childhood, Simone had pondered that problem, and witnessing of so many disappearances more than anything else corroborated these early tendencies. The death of her father, in July 1941, had not overly affected her, although she attended his last moments. The ever present danger of death for all those close to her encouraged meditation and brought her back to earlier concerns. Thus she notes, in full awareness of the mortal lot while at the same time scanning the horizon for signs of life and encouragement that are approaching: "I have written the beginning of the book which is my last and greatest recourse against death, the book I have so long desired to write; the labor of all these years may have had no other purpose than to give me the courage—and the excuse—to write it" (476).

Writing thus becomes testimony and exorcism, freeing the mind for other tasks. The philosophy teacher had tired, as she states, of teaching after twelve years. She was ready to resign from her job when a bizarre concatenation of events spared her the trouble: accused of "corrupting a minor" (Lise, who lived with young Bourla, whereas her mother wanted her to return to her former, wealthy lover and denounced Simone as the instigator of her daughter's depravity), Beauvoir was expelled from the university. She found a job as a features producer on the national radio network, which left her enough time to write. After the Liberation, she was reinstated, but never wanted to go back to teaching.

Several times in the course of the book, the author states the impossibility of giving an exact account of the war years to those who had not lived them, and yet her memoirs are a most faithful monument to those years. Setting out to write her own memoirs, keeping a diary for part of the time, Simone de Beauvoir had recreated a lively, compassionate, dramatic chronicle of the general conditions during the period that has no equal. Her integrity comes through very powerfully, as does her sense of justice. She also shows a real flair for many then unknown artists and writers. In spite of certain prejudices, certain tastes that are inevitably subjective, her perspective remains clear and straight.

CHAPTER 3

The Other Autobiographical Writings

I   La Force des Choses *(1963)* Force of Circumstance

INTENSE and vividly written, the third volume of memoirs again evokes a life dedicated to the mind, but one where social commitment has reached an active stage. Simone de Beauvoir's process of writing is never uniform but highly variable. Going to great lengths, at times, in noting explorations on distant continents, significant books and their authors, political events and the part played in them by Sartre and herself, at other times the memorialist dismisses major events, encounters, and trips in a few words. There is, of course, a system to that approach, and several times the author reveals it: whenever she felt others could speak just as well, or even better, of such experiences, she would choose brevity. In her accounts of where she went and what she did, the determining criterion for inclusion was the social significance of what should be remembered.

The whole volume, therefore, is largely oriented toward the testimony that Beauvoir wishes to deliver, whether political, intellectual, or personal. Politically, the festering sore of the Algerian War deeply marked her life; intellectually, she continued to convey a message of progress to her readers, with whom, by that time, she had established a strong bond of understanding, despite the usual insults from ideological enemies; and finally, having come to contemplate death through the irreversible process of ageing that preoccupied her more and more, she always used her own example in a way that Montaigne would not have disavowed.

Increasingly, also, she appears concerned with Sartre's well-being: he had for years abused stimulants to be able to keep up an exacting writing schedule. Several times, at home and abroad, he was near collapse, and the alarmed Simone could help and protect

him only minimally. Such crises left her self-confidence severely
jolted.

II *Existentialism as an Unwanted Label*

The third volume resumes the narration of her life where the
previous one left off, in 1944. A short preamble reports a dialogue
between the writer and her readers. Unapologetic about the
lengthiness of her narrative, Beauvoir states that she will "cut as
little as possible," this time, too,[1] as her story deserves to be heard
completely. More surprising is a statement to the effect that "certain
critics have accused me of indiscretion. It is not I who began; I
prefer rummaging through my past to leaving the task to others"
(vi). She takes pride in the general recognition of her sincerity in
memoir writing: she observed herself, she writes, "from day to day
with neither shame nor vanity" (vi–vii). What in someone else might
sound like a mere boast, in her words rings true: "I seem to my own
eyes an object, a result, without involving the notions of merit or
fault in this estimate" (vii).

After the many tasteless attacks on her earlier volumes of
memoirs, she pleads with the reader to have patience and to read
the book to the end before judging her. Then, as a dare, she declares: "I should be disappointed if [this book] failed to displease
someone. I should also be disappointed if it pleased no one . . . "
(vii). As in the Preface to *The Prime of Life*, where she admits that
her readers had pointed out to her several "small and two or three
serious" errors, she says that there may well be a few errors in the
new volume, while insisting that she never intentionally distorted
the truth.

The volume begins with a description of the Paris atmosphere
after the Liberation. Political and intellectual positions are outlined,
hopes and expectations are recalled. Simone's trip to Portugal—the
very first one after the Occupation—effects a self-confrontation in a
totally unfamiliar environment. While taking in the beauty of the
coastline and the stately buildings, as does Henri in *The Mandarins*,
the traveler focuses sharply on the misery of the common people.
The year 1945 also brings her to Tunisia, where she reveals herself
as an excellent observer of people and places with an avid and acute
perception of actual conditions.

III *The Couple*

It is in writing about this period of her life that Beauvoir has created one of the finest portrayals of the couple she and Sartre formed. Their unconventional union was bound to provoke unfriendly remarks from censorious quarters where Existentialists were viewed with distinct disfavor. Finding her name linked in punning to Sartre's name, Simone drew the line at bad taste and ill will: "Not that I was over-sensitive; when people called me 'la grande Sartreuse' or 'Notre-Dame de Sartre' I just laughed, but certain looks men gave me left their mark; looks that offered a lewd complicity with the Existentialist, and therefore dissolute, woman they took me for. To provide food for gossip, to titillate curiosity—that I did find repugnant . . . " (46).

The meaning of the word "Existentialist" brought on misunderstandings and hostility. For a time, both Sartre and Beauvoir did their best to shun the label. Eventually, the aura of dubious fame subsided. Speaking of *The Blood of Others*, critics had used the designation "resistance novel," which the author, rightly, finds wanting.

It was labeled not only a "Resistance novel" but also an "Existentialist" novel. Henceforth this label was to be affixed automatically to any work by Sartre or myself. During a discussion . . . Sartre had refused to allow Gabriel Marcel to apply this adjective to him: "My philosophy is a philosophy of existence; I don't even know what Existentialism is." I shared his irritation. I had written my novel before I had even encountered the term Existentialist; my inspiration came from my own experience, not from a system. But our protests were in vain. In the end, we took the epithet that everyone used for us and used it for our own purposes. (38)

Simone de Beauvoir shows firmness and tact in speaking of Sartre's attachment to the woman designated as "M." She gives the bare essentials of the episode, without sentimental embroiderings. Since the initial pact between the two writers left them free for adventures, there was no need for the memorialist to overemphasize this involvement. But naturally, she wanted to know how deeply Sartre was involved. "At present, their attachment was mutual, and they envisaged spending two or three months together every year. So be it: separations held no terror for me. But he evoked the weeks he had spent with her in New York with such gaiety that I grew uneasy . . ." (68–69). Simone's innate optimism "fell away." She momentarily lost her usual composure and self-confidence. It was not until Sartre had stated that though he was very fond of "M," his place was with Simone, that she regained a measure of calmness.

With their joint travels and lectures, it was only natural that Sartre and Simone should manage certain practical affairs together. Very matter of factly, Simone notes that they always shared their income, and since for a long time Sartre's was higher, that she benefited from it. When she received the Prix Goncourt, she was not so much swayed by the financial advantages it gave her as by the satisfaction of being able to contribute more to the common war chest. The prize money also enabled her to buy a studio apartment.

In the tandem Sartre-Simone de Beauvoir, she proved to be the stronger in undertaking practical arrangements and negotiations with publishers and other agencies. This becomes apparent in the way she handled the 1946 invitation by their Italian publishers to visit Italy, an invitation that pretty nearly was withdrawn for reasons of political expediency. The French had just annexed the Aosta Valley, and protests against the French were expected in the streets of major Italian cities. The publishers advised her over the telephone to postpone the trip, but Beauvoir, averse to such a cautious approach, insisted on coming. If Sartre had been on the phone, she says, he would have given in to the publishers' reasoning. Simone, who badly wanted to use up the royalties accumulated at Bompiani's, held out, and so they went.

IV A Life of Commitment—The Shadows of Ageing and Death

One of the most striking features of this third volume of memoirs is the seriousness with which Beauvoir treats the thorny problem of the bourgeois writer who is sympathetic to the proletarian masses, the miserable ones who are starving. Whereas in earlier years both Sartre and Beauvoir had been more interested in the discovery of new horizons, intellectual and geographic, now they chose to heed the call for solidarity, for help. Her compassion takes the form of an angry campaign against injustice, malnutrition, bigotry, and super-stition. Though, as noted at the beginning of the third volume, they could not be everywhere, at every demonstration or vigil, they responded readily whenever they felt their presence was urgently needed. Thus their faces became more and more familiar to the masses, as well as to the police and the newsmen. The descent from the ivory tower to the political arena demanded a great deal of time, but Beauvoir decided to pay this penalty.

Another major characteristic of this volume of memoirs is the keen awareness of ageing and of death. Throughout the book, Simone follows the inexorable process of growing old, at times with haunted melancholy, at others with a kind of resignation. More and more she thinks in terms of last opportunities: the last skiing trip, the last mountain climb, the last relationship with a man. The reader often wonders whether the author underscores ageing so strongly in order to impress others with all she is still able to do: after all, she musters an incredible amount of energy in the various extended trips she takes on several continents. She also displays uncommon energy in coping with the many demands her public stature now makes on her. Indeed, from being merely notorious before the Liberation, her and Sartre's names had now become household words, and they no longer could benefit from anonymity, whether on their travels in France or Italy or on their daily visits to Paris cafes. Simone sincerely deplores this loss of anonymity, especially in Paris, where the cafe had been a haven to both writers. Here they came to relax, to meet friends, and to work; they had spent several days there every week of their young adult lives, talking, reading, and writing. No wonder they missed the stimulating ambience. Forced to withdraw to the calm of the study, Simone de Beauvoir, for one, felt separated from the mainstream of Parisian intellectual life.

Of course, student reaction to Sartre's occasional lectures was most encouraging, and Beauvoir, too, found a warm welcome when she lectured in Paris or in Belgium. But the unique atmosphere of the cafe proved irreplaceable, a loss that was sorely felt by her.

On the other hand, readers had begun to write letters to Beauvoir, particularly after the publication of *The Second Sex* and of the first two volumes of her autobiography. In the past, her novels had generated favorable echoes, along with a number of negative ones, but now there was a regular flow of correspondence, and Simone made a point in answering most of the letters. She expresses her gratitude to her readers, whose comments were a great encouragement to her, so much more as many women volunteered that they had had experiences similar to those related both in *The Second Sex* and in the first volume of the memoirs.

V   *New Bonds—And Pangs*

When Simone de Beauvoir alights in the United States for the first time, she is fascinated with the multifaceted vast country. Although her account in *L'Amérique au Jour le Jour (America Day by Day)* is somewhat less than felicitous, because she focused excessively on nightclubs, taverns, and jazz and also proved incredibly gullible on certain college visits, there are a number of redeeming features in that volume. The impressions conveyed in the memoirs center on her personal feelings, and the encounter with Nelson Algren becomes chief among these. With total frankness and, for once, exquisite discretion, the author describes the intricate web of her relationship with Algren, in the context of her union with Jean-Paul Sartre, and necessarily also Sartre's attachment both to her—calmly, solidly, unquestioningly—and to "M"—passionately, but without, on his part, the same feeling of permanence.

From the outset, Simone's relationship with Algren suffered from the limitations she had set because of her attachment to Sartre. Although Algren had understood the warning, it had not been clear to him how uncertain their future was to be; on Simone's part, also, reality and ideas clashed, and with all her firm intentions, she could not at all times master her life as well as she thought she could: "during those two months at Miller, I had shifted from stupefied unbelief to resignation. It didn't hurt any more. But every once in a while a void would open up inside of me; it was as though my life were coming to a stop. I would look at Saint-Germain-des-Prés: there would be nothing behind it. Once my heart had beat in other places at the same time; now I was where I was, there and nowhere else. What austerity!" (p. 245)

When the break with Algren came, it was a shock to her. On his side, it was rather a defensive move: he could not stand the constant uncertainty and the recurrent separations. The break did not prevent them from remaining close friends, and Algren was to visit Simone in Europe. But at the moment, Simone was in a somber mood:

I had buried my memories of Chicago a second time, and they no longer caused me pain—but what sadness to feel the pain subside! "Well, that's that," I said to myself; and I no longer even thought about my happiness with Algren. Less inclined than ever to what are called adventures, my age and the circumstances of my life left little room, it seemed, for a new love. My body, perhaps as a result of a deeply ingrained pride, adapts easily; it made no demands. But there was something in me that would not submit to such indifference. "I'll never sleep again warmed by another's body." Never: what a knell! When the realization of these facts penetrated me, I felt myself sinking into death. (254)

While the portrayal of the intercontinental couple in *The Mandarins* did not lack warmth or depth of feeling, a certain casual tone may have caused uneasiness in some readers: Anne seemed too harsh, too determined, and Lewis was not given enough backbone. He might appear just a moody, capricious weakling. The real people are shown to suffer in the memoirs, and such candor makes up for the potential cynicism of the novelistic treatment. To conclude the interrupted quotation:

The void had always frightened me, but till now I had been dying day by day without paying attention to it; suddenly, at one blow, a whole piece of myself was being engulfed before my eyes; it was like some brutal but inexplicable amputation, for nothing had happened to me. In the glass my face still looked the same; behind me a burning past was still not far away, but, in the long years stretching ahead of me, it would not flame up again; it would never flame up again. I suddenly found myself on the other side of a line, though there was no one moment when I had crossed it. . . . (254)

This fine analysis is made with all the insight that the novelist brings to bear on her own life. It is a moving lament on lost youth. Yet, the woman who here took leave of her active life was to be surprised once more: all the seemingly objective assessments of her ageing, isolation, and detachment did not keep her from being sought, some time later, by a young man, and years of good companionship were to be added to her life as a woman.

VI   *A Reminder of Frailty*

Simone de Beauvoir had witnessed the amazingly rapid decline of the woman who typed her manuscripts for her, Lucienne Baudin. Afflicted with a breast cancer, diagnosed too late, she had died miserably, after a long and agonizing treatment. When Simone felt a lump in her breast, the physician recommended a biopsy. What haunted Simone was the vision of her secretary's rapid deterioration and death. When her own growth was found to be benign, she felt immense relief. In her constant awareness of mortality, Simone was deeply impressed by this episode and recorded it perceptively.

Keeping her life separate from her writing, the novelist nonetheless allows major themes of her own experience to become interwoven at times in her fiction. Thus when Beauvoir in her memoirs reflects on the composition of *The Mandarins,* insisting how much care went into the shaping of various characters, particularly women, she enables us to observe the slow process of "decanting" from life, selecting traits that ought to make her protagonists more lifelike without stamping them as recognizable by name: "all the material I drew from memory was refracted, diluted, hammered thin, blown up, mixed, transposed, twisted, sometimes completely reversed, and in every case re-created. I would have liked people to take this book for what it is: neither autobiography, nor reportage: an evocation" (269–70). It may not be an especially new discovery to see a writer at work, painstakingly and scrupulously creating her own world. But such notations confirm the deep sense of professional dedication to be found in Beauvoir's work. While she rarely comments on the creative process in painters, for example, her sense of métier is keenly alive at all times, and she strives to fulfill her mission. That was an early drive in the "dutiful daughter"; it remains in the mature artist.

VII   *African Tour*

Simone de Beauvoir was to experience a shock of another kind. Several times, she had gone to Spain and to North Africa. When it seemed politically advisable for Sartre to contact African nationalists on their own continent, Simone joined in the planned expedition. Politically, however, this trip proved to be frustrating, as French Communists had warned the Africans not to contact Sartre. But on many grounds, the discovery of a part of the world entirely new to her yielded fruitful experiences. Her keen gift of observation combines with her fundamental humanism to reveal an Africa which, though a tourist's view, contains many perceptive notations. The colonial French society with its unbelievable conservatism is shown concretely: in deepest Africa the French women dress exactly as in Romorantin. The men with their drinking and their basic contempt for Africans are described fleetingly, in some cases sympathetically; these descriptions became more caustic after the Paris tabloids pub-

lished lurid and scandalous versions of her and Sartre's African expedition. Yet, all in all, the tone of the account of the African journey differs profoundly from other descriptions where the writer was
more positively involved, as in the Brazilian travelogue.

VIII *New Friendships, Loss of Old Ones*

Through her political involvement, Simone de Beauvoir made
many new acquaintances. In a few cases, these encounters became
lasting friendships. She notes scrupulously how often Sartre and she
were called upon to join the protest against the Algerian War and
various other political demonstrations. Taken singly, the descriptions of protest marches are confused and leave an impression of
complete amateurism in the organization of these movements,
which actually demanded much care and planning—though, often
enough, last minute changes became necessary when the police
blocked essential access roads. The details of the demonstrations
read like a juvenile story, full of enthusiasm, of nodding to familiar
faces, of name dropping. Yet, paradoxically, there emerges through
the frequently confused accounts, the graphic impression of a totality that has become part and parcel of history: a clear picture of our
time emerges from pages that are full of descriptive chaos; no wonder Simone depicted some demonstrations where she felt like the
Stendhalian hero at the battle of Waterloo.

While new friendships developed through the mutual bond of
struggling for peace, the ties to Camus broke over the controversy
fostered by *The Rebel*, of which Francis Jeanson had written a devastating review in Sartre's *Les Temps Modernes*. Neither side was
blameless, but Beauvoir makes it appear that Camus aggravated the
case by taking the criticism so personally and formalizing his complaint in a letter addressed to Sartre as director of *TM*.

Force of Circumstance contains a description of Camus by
Beauvoir that is far more complex than earlier portrayals. The
good-natured drinking companion of the war and postwar years who
sometimes confided in Simone is now sharply criticized for his failure to speak up during the Algerian War. His anti-Communism
caused Camus to espouse attitudes that his old friends found unac-
ceptable. Conversely, Camus felt slighted when Sartre's associates
tore *The Rebel* to pieces. But the shock of the announcement of
Camus' death, in January 1960, affected Sartre and Beauvoir
deeply, and that whole night long they reminisced on their relation-

ship with him. Unable to sleep, Simone got up and went out to walk the streets of Paris:

It wasn't the fifty-year-old man I was mourning; not that just man without justice, so arrogant and touchy behind his stern mask, who had been struck out of my heart when he gave his approval to the crimes of France; it was the companion of our hopeful years, whose open face laughed and smiled so easily, the young ambitious writer, wild to enjoy life, its pleasures, its triumphs, and comradeship, friendship, love and happiness. Death had brought him back to life; for him, time no longer existed, yesterday had no more truth now than the day before; Camus as I had loved him emerged from the night about me, in the same instant recovered and painfully lost. (484)

IX A Stranger in Her Own Country

The break with Camus had come about for complex reasons; an estrangement had been felt by Beauvoir for quite some time before the open break occurred. In the ensuing years, Camus' espousal of the French nationalist point of view had increased the distance that existed between them. Increasingly, as the Algerian War intensified, the formerly aloof intellectual resented the dilemma in which she saw herself placed: as a native Frenchwoman, she felt solidary with the fate of her country. When atrocities were committed in the name of France, her shock was profound and lasting: she felt removed from national life and uncomfortable in the presence of her fellow countrymen. After returning from abroad, she would shudder with revulsion every time she overheard some crude, crassly nationalistic remark. As long as the conflict lasted, she tried to spend her vacations abroad, because the daily contact with the average Frenchman had become painful to her, whereas the Italians, having lost their colonies, shared her feelings toward the aspirations for independence voiced by the Algerians.

In part, her violent reactions and new militancy stem from her regret at realizing so slowly the urgency of the cause. As late as 1958, upon returning from Italy, she admits that she cannot very well "go around mimicking [Sartre] all the time."—"I blame myself for not having tried to do more. . . .When I come back from Italy I'll try to commit myself more actively. I should find the present situation less intolerable if I had been more energetic and militant . . ." (407).

Basically, Beauvoir felt she was not a woman of action: "my reason for living is writing; to sacrifice that I would have to believe myself indispensable in some other field" (461). In this, however, she was mistaken; while some of her friends did much more than she did, Simone found satisfaction in living according to her own taste, following her vocation. Her sense of being divorced from the mainstream of French public life is strong throughout the Algerian crisis. In brief, precise strokes, Beauvoir succeeds in demonstrating the unbelievable inconsistencies of French governmental policy toward Algeria in the late fifties and early sixties. With equal accuracy she gives a thumbnail sketch of her and Sartre's position in a France ruined by crude nationalism: "We had begun by loathing a few men and a few factions; little by little we were made forcibly aware that all our fellow countrymen were accomplices in this crime and that we were exiles in our own country. There were only a very few of us who did not join in the general chorus. We were accused of demoralizing the nation" (340).

The abuse does not remain purely verbal: as Algerian independence becomes a concrete possibility, bombs are thrown. Besides the editorial offices of *Esprit* and other liberal publications, Sartre's house is attacked. Sartre and Beauvoir go into hiding. From cautious beginnings—disagreement with Francis Jeanson's support of the Algerian rebels, revulsion at the use of torture by the French, and indignation at the monumental indifference of the majority of Frenchmen—Sartre and Beauvoir moved toward espousal of the principle of Algerian independence and urged an early end to the war. In so doing, they separated themselves from the mainstream of French politics. Even some liberals around *L'Express* were hesitant about going that far: fully committed partisans of an end to French rule in Algeria for a long time went against the grain of national feeling.

For the whole duration of that unholy conflict, Simone de Beauvoir suffered in her position as a French thinker and writer and simply as a French citizen. Whenever she came in touch with "ordinary" people, her sense of justice, of fairness, was wounded through the vulgar oversimplification that equated everything French with impeccable goodness, everything Algerian with barbarity. American opponents of the war in Vietnam felt similar pangs during the trying years of the Far Eastern involvement of the United States. Few Frenchmen had ever felt so lonely as Sartre and Beauvoir in their tireless fight against the manifestations of blind nationalism. Their

predicament is reminiscent of Romain Rolland's position at the outset of World War I, when he was isolated from French national
attitudes during his long solitary struggle against imperialism both
in Germany and in his own country.

The cathartic experience of her ostracism made Beauvoir into a
more thoughtfully committed writer. Whereas she had unreservedly enjoyed life before the Algerian War, even in the midst of the
material and political pressures during the German Occupation,
there was hardly any relief for her during the Algerian crisis. Not
surprisingly, she had to take a vacation abroad now and then to
escape the ever-present stifling atmosphere she sensed in France.

No doubt her choice of continuing to write her memoirs was
partly determined by a certain need to justify herself. Owing to the
success of her earlier memoirs with a broad segment of the public,
she may have believed that the undecided might drop their prejudice and frame a new, more forward-looking political view
through her influence. Naturally, Beauvoir could not have direct
"electioneering" in mind, since by the time the third volume of her
memoirs was published, the Algerian War had finally subsided. But
the disappointment she had felt was deep and lasting, and she
wanted Frenchmen to know about it.

The sense of shame at being French when Frenchmen condoned
torture in Algeria—and in France, too, for that matter—was mitigated by the feeling of elated, fraternal happiness experienced during mass protest marches against police for shooting demonstrators.
However, as soon as the elation wore off, she would be haunted by
distressing thoughts of her own responsibility for the national dis-
grace. Even the end of the war in Algeria did not bring immediate
relief from this oppressive state, for Simone knew that other injustices remained. She was determined to fight them, but the unending struggle proved taxing and at times discouraging.

X Simone de Beauvoir, Pioneer Feminist

It was natural, having written *The Second Sex* and being praised
both by women and other supporters of her point of view, as well as
abused by what she calls "la chiennerie spécifiquement française"
(translated variably and correctly by "bitchiness," "meanness" (186,
187)—although the translation cannot convey the full extent of de-
grading vulgarity implied), that Beauvoir should continue to speak
out for women's causes. One might take her outspoken position for

granted, but that would overlook the fact that the writer had no
apparent need to pursue a battle that, as far as she personally was
concerned, had been won:

> I was never treated as a target for sarcasm until after *The Second Sex:*
> before that, people were either indifferent or kind to me. Afterward, I was
> often attacked as a woman because my attackers thought it must be my
> Achilles' heel; but I knew perfectly well that this persistent petulance was
> really aimed at my moral and social convictions. No, far from suffering from
> my femininity, I have, on the contrary, from the age of twenty on, accumu-
> lated the advantages of both sexes; after *She Came to Stay,* those around me
> treated me both as a writer, their peer in the masculine world, and as a
> woman; this was particularly noticeable in America . . . . (189)

Her frankness in acknowledging such a privileged position shields
Beauvoir against certain reproaches that might be directed at her
by women. She did not, after all, have to suffer through the ordinary
frustration of women trying to assert themselves in a man's world.
But since she can hardly be accused of asserting herself at the
expense of other women, why and how should she renounce a
privileged position in this imperfectly integrated society?

XI *Premature Abdication*

At several junctures in the third volume of memoirs, Beauvoir
voices regret over the loss of vigor in the pursuit of her tasks.
Whereas she used to enjoy climbing mountains, she now prefers
driving; while she still enjoys traveling, fatigue at times takes its toll.
Ageing has set in, and a sometimes morosely resigned woman recognizes the futility of all human endeavors. So it comes as a complete
surprise to her when a man in his twenties invites her to go to the
movies—any movies. As she was forty-four, she no longer expected
that a new close relationship with a man was possible. Discreet but
firm, the account of her attachment to Lanzmann shows a new kind
of insight and conveys feeling through omission rather than exact
notation. The predominant factor is the perfect ease with which
Sartre and Simone adjust to the new companionship. Various trips
taken together with Sartre and Michèle Vian—his new friend—and
renewed travels attest the viability of the foursome.

The friendship with Lanzmann brought Simone happiness as a
woman while confirming her in her intellectual pursuits. More

serene as far as her life was concerned, she engaged as vigorously as
ever in her writing and in meeting her political commitments.
Travel became easier after Lanzmann shared the driving with her,
and his considerable journalistic experience helped Simone get essential information for her research. But apart from practical considerations and the mutually beneficial exchange of ideas, theirs
proved to be a most congenial relationship; Lanzmann's thoughtful
attention and devotion were deeply gratifying to her. Whenever he
circled the globe on one of his journalistic assignments, to Israel, to
Korea, he would wire and call her whenever possible. As Sartre was
involved with Michèle Vian at about the same time, the arrangement worked out satisfactorily: during vacation time, the four of
them would travel in Italy or Greece, sometimes in pairs.

When, after about six years, the relationship came to an end,
Simone noted it with a sort of fatalistic detachment. She felt old age
was setting in; everything else contributed to her moroseness, it was
a bad year that ended just then. Still, with all the bitter aftertastes,
Beauvoir manages to write about these disappointments from a certain distance and without personal recriminations. Active and
energetic in her attitude to the outside world, she proved strong
enough to master the crisis. Unlike the break with Nelson Algren,
the change from a very close relationship with Lanzmann to a good
but more distant friendship seems to have remained without bitter
feeling on either side.

Her writing offered sorely needed moral support: she was vigorously pursuing the completion of a volume of memoirs at the time.
What she said about the first volume of these memoirs applies as
much as ever: "since it has been published and read, the story of my
childhood and youth has detached itself from me entirely" (463).
Similarly, the painful readjustment after Lanzmann dropped out of
her life could be made successfully thanks to her concentration on
the rendering of other portions of her life. Writing was, in part, a
therapy for her.

XII *Credulity*

The author of *The Second Sex* had proven to be shrewd in her
selection of materials for inclusion in the documentation. The literary essayist was careful in the preparation of her essay on Sade. So it
comes as something of a shock to the reader of the memoirs—and

occasionally of some parts of the travelogues, too—when Beauvoir straightfacedly gives some information, or quotes others as
giving information, that strains the belief of the reader.

Had she as much as suggested a smile, we would not stumble over
such tall tales as the cure for a certain parasite in Central Africa.
Reading the bare facts as the author states them, one cannot help
but frown at such utter credulity: "Bamako and the surrounding
districts teem with frightful diseases. There are long worms that find
their way through the skin on the soles of the feet and dig caves
inside for themselves; to get them out, you have to get hold of one
and roll it tight around a matchstick; you give the matchstick a turn
every day; it's no good trying to pull it out all at once because it
would break and then you'd never get rid of it . . . " (221).

One cannot ask of traveling writers to control medical facts. One
might hope they would bolster their stories by some authority that
would go some way toward making the story plausible.

Likewise, without the slightest hint of a smile, the memorialist
gives an account of Iceland and its drinking problems: "The Ice-
landers are hard drinkers; they were capable of making alcohol out
of shoe polish. The principal task of the police was to pick the drunks
out of the gutters at night" (248).

Sometimes, it is true, the author does not assume direct responsibility for relaying such incredible stories. In an interview with Han
Suyin, Beauvoir listens to descriptions of the new China and of
certain Chinese settlements outside China: "She told me that in
Singapore and even in Canton, despite the new regime, there are
still communities of women (about thirty thousand in Canton) who
are officially recognized as Lesbians; they marry within the community and adopt children. They may leave the community and
marry a man. In that case they cut their hair" (450).

Without some sociological comment or element of comparison,
such statements contravene the standards of serious research. It
would be necessary to weigh such stories against other reports on
similar conditions or to furnish elements of information concerning
the general situation in Singapore and in Canton. Without such
elements of comparison, one must doubt the veracity of the statement. Simone de Beauvoir also showed her credulousness on her
trip to the United States, when she uncritically wrote what she had
been told about some women's colleges. To her, these may have

seemed trivial details. The reader may think her careless or naive but, as a matter of fact, she is generally careful to document her claims in all essentials.

XIII   The Best of Simone de Beauvoir

The memorialist is at her best when she describes her two months' stay in Brazil; the account is colorful, psychologically vivid, and full of sharply observed detail. The Brazilian tour was not a frivolous pleasure tour or a hasty excursion, nor does the travelogue focus on her meeting with intellectuals. Though she describes Brazilian writers, architects, politicians, and artists at length, Simone de Beauvoir devotes most of her attention to the vast country and its astounding contrasts: modern buildings and ancient superstitions, Marxist aspirations interwoven with Afro-American cults and dances, racial intermixtures and racist dispositions in a society still very much in flux. The author succeeds in giving a lively, intriguing, stimulating picture of her visit in a South America seen to be in turmoil. It was fitting, therefore, that Sartre and she should have ended their trip by a short return visit to Cuba, where they found things much changed from their first visit. Though treated as honored guests, they perceived a marked deterioration in the intellectual climate; this deterioration was confirmed by friends, who subsequently reported to them on measures taken by Castro to remedy the decline.

Open-minded and alert on their travels to China (1956), the Soviet Union (1956, 1962, and several years thereafter), and Japan (1966), Sartre and Beauvoir were able to put their observation to good use in their prolonged struggle for peace through various organizations. Though often attacked by French Communist Party stalwarts, they managed to maintain a staunch political independence. Writers of the left, they were increasingly respected, even by Communists, for their undaunted, consistent efforts on behalf of causes that should at all times have commanded left-wing solidarity but often failed to do so. Unfailingly allied to the parties representing social progress, Sartre and Beauvoir succeeded in creating a middle ground on which to work and fight for substantially the same causes without ever becoming beholden to party orthodoxy and rigid dogma.

It has been said, rightly, that the work of both authors was somewhat limited in its ideological scope by their belonging, through their family origins and their upbringing, to the middle classes. Neither of them ever denied that it was so; on the contrary, repeatedly, in word and deed (in their essays and speeches as well as their fiction and drama), they evoked people feeling just as they felt, separated from the working class but in essential sympathy with it, identifying with its goals, fighting its fights. Needless to add, it takes courage and consistency, in view of the constant opposition from Communists, to maintain an attitude of consistency in their fundamental support of left-wing causes and to overcome the temptation of giving up on proletarian causes altogether.

XIV *Profits and Losses as Seen in* Force of Circumstance

The third volume of the memoirs contains glowing accounts of intellectual excitement over the creative process. It gives precise insight into rehearsals where Simone felt involved. The travelogues alternate between trivial and sometimes superficial notations on some trips to North Africa, Scandinavia, and elsewhere, and gripping evocations of human misery on other explorations of the globe. The volume recounts in vivid detail the political evolution of the author, who was slow in joining her friends in their fight against injustice and totalitarianism but, once moved to act, remained a steadfast member of the protest front. There are pages of moving beauty and pages of rather cut and dried narrative on the circumstances under which certain of Sartre's or her own books were written. All in all, the volume stands as a remarkable monument to the crucial years of the cold war and of some major crises in French and world politics and to the part played therein by a number of French intellectuals. It is written with the writer's heart blood and therefore creates a kind of communication which is very rare: a whole era, with its ups and downs, its hopes and disillusionments, is seen through the temperament of a highly gifted writer.

The very end of the volume has been largely misinterpreted, according to the author, who had written these concluding words: "the promises had all been kept. And yet, turning an incredulous gaze toward that young and credulous girl [herself], I realized with stupor how much I was gypped" (658). This was widely interpreted as signifying a profound disillusionment in a woman who had been deceived and frustrated by life. Not so, says the author repeatedly, perhaps most emphatically in the ensuing volume of memoirs: "That expression, 'I was gypped' does not refer to the last few pages of the book. It is, rather, to be explained [by the encounter] not so much by my reflection in the mirror as by my rebellion, my anguished rebellion against the horrors of this world: comparing this world to the dreams of my adolescence, I finally saw how deeply I had been deceived."[2]

Whether one accepts this elaborate explanation or not, Simone de Beauvoir chose, or tried, to obliterate an expression of disillusionment and to offer a more circumstantial version of her disgust: all the world is a farce, a place of deceptive illusions. That is what one ought to rebel against. Such a position could not be a strong assertion in view of the author's lifelong optimism. It should be noted for the sake of contrast. The author's work as a totality will tell us more assuredly where she stands.

XV   Une Mort Très Douce (1964) A Very Easy Death

The relationship between Simone and her mother, as one has seen from *Memoirs of a Dutiful Daughter*, was far from easy. For many years during her childhood and adolescence, Simone had been in outright rebellion against her mother who, afraid that her younger daughter, Hélène, might be perverted through her elder's influence, tried to discourage the sisters' intimacy. Subsequently, the bitter feelings of Madame de Beauvoir toward her rebellious daughter were mitigated by the latter's literary success.

One day, in October 1963, while in Rome, Simone de Beauvoir received a telephone call from Paris: her friend Bost told her that her mother had had an accident. She had slipped in the bathroom and broken her hip bone. Rushing to her mother's bedside, Simone found her reasonably comfortable. Her hip would heal without an operation, in a matter of three months. But a history of intestinal complications caused the physicians to make more tests. They found a cancerous growth, and from that moment on it was merely a question of how long Simone's mother would have to suffer.

Simone pleaded with one of the doctors to avoid senseless, hopeless suffering, but ran into a stone wall. The doctor repeated over and over again: "I will do what I have to do. . . ." No wonder Simone's thoughts came to focus on euthanasia. What amazed both Simone and her sister was the mother's determination to live and her confident attitude. Although a night nurse had been hired, the sisters took turns staying with their mother overnight, relieving each other. The thought of any more nightmares upsetting Françoise became intolerable to both daughters. They spelled each other for the thirty days that the agony lasted.

In retrospect, Simone sheds some more light on her mother's youth. A rather unhappy child, Françoise had welcomed marriage enthusiastically and no doubt found the first ten to fifteen years of her marriage happy. But, frustrated over his material failures, tradition-bound, and embittered, her husband had become more and more authoritarian and, also, had more and more neglected his wife, running to cafes every night, sometimes staying away from home. No wonder, writes the daughter, that Françoise de Beauvoir tried to live for her children and thereby actually lived through them, asserting her rather unbending authority over the years of their youth.

When her husband died, in 1941, Françoise de Beauvoir had quickly adjusted to the necessity of making a living: she trained herself and became a librarian for a time. Even when she no longer needed the small income she could make independently, she continued to serve on a voluntary basis in libraries and community services. She created a new circle of friends for herself and led a life of relative fulfillment.

Her religious attachments always were strong, and while she was in the clinic, supposedly for a broken hip, her friends assailed both daughters with constantly renewed requests to have their mother see a priest. But Françoise de Beauvoir never expressed such a desire; hence both daughters felt fully justified in refusing, which caused furious accusations. In the end, Françoise had "a very easy death," according to a night nurse, without having received the last rites.

The book, *A Very Easy Death*, attains a strangely moving quality in the simple recital of events, sometimes intertwined with retrospective remarks. We find a Simone de Beauvoir miles removed from intellectual preoccupations, seeking to relieve her mother's anxiety, physically comforting her, scolding her when she made defeatist remarks, encouraging her in every way. Was it bad conscience that made her fit so completely into the pattern of the small duties family members fulfill whenever one of theirs is seriously ill? Rather than a guilty conscience, it seems, Simone's fascination with the problem of death and dying brought her closer to her mother again. She had seen her mother regularly when she was well and always wrote her. Material matters did not count, in Simone's eyes, and it was only

natural that she should have used some of the income from her
books to help her mother whenever she could.

The poor, aching body of her mother, so frail, so vulnerable,
made Simone realize more intensely than any philosophical speculation the nearness of death. She had been haunted by images and
thoughts of death ever since her childhood, so the new discoveries
merely confirmed earlier reflections. However, the revolt felt by
Simone stemmed from outrage at what seemed to her senseless
suffering: while her mother probably still derived some pleasure
from the short respite procured through the life-sustaining ap-
paratus, on balance Simone felt the pain was costing more than this
rather shabby advantage was worth.

XVI   A Whole Gamut of Contradictory Emotions

Simone noted her first reactions when she heard of the hazards
her mother was exposed to in lying motionless over a period of three
months while her hip bone was to heal: "I was not very much
affected. In spite of her frailty my mother was tough. And after all,
she was of an age to die."[3] Over the weeks of her mother's confinement, Simone's attitude changed profoundly. She no longer was
sure there is an "age to die"—"the words were devoid of meaning,
as so many words are. For the first time I saw her as a dead body
under a suspended sentence" (20).

As to her mother's religious beliefs, which were supposed to make
dying easier, Simone finds that "she believed in heaven, but in spite
of her age, her feebleness and her poor health, she clung ferociously
to this world, and she had an animal dread of death" (14). When the
mother, feeling slightly better, expressed reluctance at the idea of
returning to the studio apartment she had lived in since her husband's death, twenty years ago, Simone soothed her by promising
she would not have to return there ever. If she was averse to envisage dying with equanimity, Françoise de Beauvoir accepted old age
easily. With every slight improvement, she made plans for the future, ready to "start a fresh chapter" (17).

Wondering how she came to adjust to her role of attending her
mother, Simone "realized that [my] mother's accident was affecting
me far more than I had thought it would. I could not really see why.
It had wrenched her out of the framework, the role, the set of
images in which I had imprisoned her: I recognized her in this
patient in bed, but I did not recognize either the pity or the kind of
disturbance that she aroused in me" (21).

Once cancer was diagnosed, the sisters alternated between hopes that their mother "would not get through the day" and the prospect of renewed agony raised by the amazingly vigorous remissions. They wished to spare her the pain and despair of suffering knowingly. Wandering through the whitened corridors of the clinic, Simone wondered what pitiful dramas might be going on behind the closed doors. "From now on one of these dramas belonged to me" (44).

During the many hours that her mother lay sleeping or at best semiconscious, Simone was able to muse about her mother's life. She saw her compensating for her frustrations by asserting her control over her daughters. Her "heavy-handed intrusions" into the lives of the young she judged "clumsy," and yet the ambivalence in her feelings toward her daughters struck Simone as inevitable. However, she considered her mother's unhappiness to be partly of her own doing: "Thinking against oneself often bears fruit; but with my mother it was another question again—she *lived* against herself" (42). By that expression, Simone de Beauvoir means to point to the impossibility facing Françoise in trying to overcome the norms, rules, and taboos of her upbringing.

Rather rigid and unbending during her independent life, Françoise de Beauvoir, under the pressure of illness, became less stubborn. When one of her nurses was evicted, she readily agreed to let her use her own apartment, all the more readily as she had determined to move anyway. "Her illness had quite broken the shell of her prejudices and pretensions: perhaps because she no longer needed these defences" (60).

When her mother seemed to improve at one moment, Simone decided to go ahead with her plans, and she flew to Prague with Sartre. Called back earlier than expected, because her mother had said to Hélène, "I shall not see Simone again," the dutiful daughter pondered what makes us react to death the way we do.

I did not particularly want to see maman again before her death; but I could not bear the idea that she should not see me again. Why attribute such importance to a moment since there would be no memory? There would not be any atonement either. For myself I understood, to the innermost fibre of my being, that the absolute could be enclosed within the last moments of a dying person. (62–63)

While waiting outside her mother's door, Simone had ample time to live again the years of relative tension between her mother and herself. She recalled how, when *Memoirs of a Dutiful Daughter* had appeared, in 1958, she had taken a bunch of flowers to her mother, with a mere word of apology, and had seen her mother moved and astonished. Françoise de Beauvoir later remarked: "Parents do not understand their children, but it works both ways" (69).

Seeing the increasing deterioration in her mother's physical condition, Simone became calmer: "The transition from my mother to a living corpse had been definitively accomplished. The world had shrunk to the size of her room: when I crossed Paris in a taxi I saw nothing more than a stage with extras walking about on it. My real life took place at her side, and it had only one aim—protecting her" (73).

The necessary concentration on the most immediate functioning of vital organs which attends a watch over illness caused Simone to change her perspective on humans for a time. "I Looked at people with a fresh eye, obsessed by the complicated system of tubes that was concealed under their clothing. Sometimes I myself turned into a lift-and-force pump or into a sequence of pockets and guts" (74). Obsessive thoughts were understandably frequent at the time, but they did not remain with Simone, unless one considers her systematic study of old people obsessive—which it is not. Though her interest was certainly sparked by what happened to her mother, the study coincided with profound preoccupations throughout her life as a writer.

Simone de Beauvoir suspected hypocrisy everywhere. Now, she herself had to use little lies to humor her mother. Both her sister and she were near nervous exhaustion on account of the constant fear and pressure. As she put it, "What tried us more than anything were maman's death-agonies, her resurrections, and our own inconsistency. In this race between pain and death we most earnestly hoped that death would come first" (75). Yet, at the same time, they were afraid of the last breath that would make the separation irreparable.

Despite her suffering, Françoise de Beauvoir showed a tenacious will to live. For Simone, most hours, most instants were "pointless torment" (81). When the mother laments the loss of wakeful moments, having slept many hours during the day, it strikes Simone with overwhelming clarity that this is the incipient revolt against death: " 'Today I haven't lived.'—'I am losing days.' Every day had an irreplaceable value for her. And she was going to die. She did not know it: but I did. In her name, I revolted against it" (83).

Françoise de Beauvoir died without having seen a priest, and her daughters realized that this had spared her a moment's fear. For fear of death and religion go hand in hand. Neither Simone nor Hélène could help thinking what would have happened if, mercifully, their mother had died on the day of the operation. "We did derive an undoubted good from this respite: it saved us, or almost saved us, from remorse. When someone you love dies you pay for the sin of outliving her with a thousand piercing regrets. Her death brings to light her unique quality; she grows as vast as the world that her absence annihilates for her . . . you feel that she should have had more room in your life . . ." (94).

The sisters simply and spontaneously agreed on the funeral ceremony. Simone speaks for both in saying: "We were taking part in the dress rehearsal for our own burial" (99–100).

Wondering why her mother's death shook her so profoundly, Simone came to the conclusion that the various aspects of her mother's personality had fused into one. "The 'Maman darling' of the days when I was ten can no longer be told from the inimical woman who oppressed my adolescence; I wept for them both when I wept for my old mother. I thought I had made up my mind about our failure and accepted it; but its sadness comes back to my heart" (103).

XVII *Revelations through the Nearness of Death*

Looking back on this little book with its simple narrative, one notes that Simone de Beauvoir considers herself as living in a show-case. Anything having to do with her or her family belongs in the public domain and is described without apparent passion. Her voice is that of the chronicler who transmits facts to future generations. Thus it may seem that, when recording the accident, the sub-sequent hospitalization, and the medical treatment, the author foregoes a human reaction in *A Very Easy Death*. When opinions are expressed, the tone changes immediately. Her mother at one moment uttered words "that froze me. . . . Telling me of her night at the Boucicaut [hospital] she said 'You know what the women of the lower classes are like: they moan' " (19).

In general, Beauvoir's attitude toward death and dying was pro-foundly modified through the harrowing experience of seeing her mother decline and die within a matter of weeks. Graphically, but also sensitively, the memorialist recorded her own step by step adaptation to the changing daily necessities of comfort and attendant care. Whereas Simone's life had centered on political and intellectual problems, now the more immediate concern with bodily comfort predominated. Her sense of priorities was affected by the encounter with death, causing her to adopt a more lenient attitude toward many less pressing problems. Most of her writing since that period is directed toward fundamental human problems, and while social and political questions still count and must be solved and her leadership role in the fight against injustice remains as firm as ever, the more urgent need is for readiness to accept old age and death. Simone's whole outlook has changed. She appears more serene in her thinking about death and dying.

From the beginning, most of Beauvoir's writings, above all her autobiographical books, show the central preoccupation with death. In reading a whole book dedicated substantially to the death of her mother, the reader might expect an atmosphere of gloom, of unmitigated meditation on death. That this is not so is perhaps the greatest surprise in this beautiful memorial to Simone's mother. In her review of the book, Elizabeth Janeway—not a lenient critic of Beauvoir—comments on this phenomenon, declaring that she is not sure why this book is not at all unbearable to read. She concludes:

One can only say . . . that the dignity and indeed the nobility of this book is explicable by its humanity alone. There are no clues because there are no tricks, no justification, no moralizing. This woman lived and died, this is how the arc of her life bowed down into the grave. Why are not the details of her pain painful, the glimpses of her fear frightening? Why is this story of a death illuminating and enlarging? I don't know. That is the secret of art, never to be spelled out, but here once more figured forth.[4]

Similarly, from a Catholic religious point of view, Pierre-Henri Simon ponders on what makes the attraction of this book. He had expected to be repelled by a certain dogmatic didacticism which, he thought, prevailed in many of Beauvoir's essays. Such attitudes, he felt, "made one wonder whether there could even be a residual tenderness and feminine emotivity, wanting at times in the author of *The Second Sex*, even the author of *Force of Circumstance*, and *The Mandarins*."[5]

But, he discovers, "at the bedside of her mother, Simone de Beauvoir is a daughter who is naturally suffering. Her intelligence and her habits of rational thinking do not at all tend to paralyze her affectivity; they rather serve to universalize the significance of suffering. Perhaps here she gave if not the best of herself, at least the innermost secret, the most spontaneous, the least altered by any philosophical refractions."[6]

How, then, is it possible that a book on dying tells us so much more about Simone de Beauvoir herself than it does of her mother or even of death and dying? Simply because the author does not conceal the central interest she takes in observing every step her mother takes toward death. Even though the observation is cushioned by compassion, the writer at all times preserves her lucidity. It is the death of her mother, an event that touches her own life rather deeply; and yet, despite her ardent plea with one of the doctors when she still believed her mother's suffering might be abbreviated, Beauvoir remains calm, rational, simply a chronicler.

The penalty the professional writer must pay is perhaps that even intimate letters from his or her life will find their way into print. Likewise, journals, whether meant for posterity or not, are never safe from inquisitive eyes. No account, however private, is exempt from public scrutiny. Still, here we have something quite unique: an intimate event, observed from the bedside of the dying mother and presented for all to share, not so much for its literary interest— which is undeniable—but as a matter of conscience: the daughter continues her dutiful life in recording for mankind this intimate experience, describing it to the best of her ability, in order to create a monument for her mother, to be sure, but also as an example for others to live and die by.

Simone de Beauvoir has created this monument, and it may help others envisage death with less fear. What had been foremost in her mind, though, had been the mere recital of simple human relations: she demonstrated her concern for the well-being of her mother; she comforted her and helped her, together with her sister, die without fear. Thus others may derive comfort and solace from this memorial, even though it remains the private record of one particular death.

XVIII   Tout Compte Fait *(1972)* All Said and Done

Few of Simone de Beauvoir's books have been left completely unscathed by critics. Even her most successful novels and journals, while acclaimed by the vast majority, provoked some negative reac-

tions. But none of her books reaped anything like the almost unani-
mously negative reviews that followed the publication of *All Said
and Done*. The critics were especially displeased with her chapter
on dreams and her frequent synopses of books and movies. "Trite,"
"uninteresting" were among the less unfavorable epithets hurled at
the author who was said to be "finished," "extinct," and who had
apparently disappointed her readers.

And yet, the volume, which does have lengthy descriptions of
matters not of primary interest to everyone, also contains important
statements by the author regarding her attitudes toward some fundamental problems, such as religion. She notes the changes in her
and, more often, the permanence in her outlook. What adds, in my
view, to the definite value of the book are the sequels to earlier
portraits of friends and acquaintances: in most cases, a tragic touch is
added to what was told earlier. Almost without exception, these are
lives out of the ordinary. Granted, there are certain cliches in the
volume, as for instance the cavalier treatment of the various important trips to distant continents. These are described in an often
impersonal, traveloguelike way and do not differ markedly from
what one might expect one's friends to bring back for a home slide
show from such places as Japan or Sweden.

But even some of these accounts have relief and personality, and
their political significance is practically always convincing. It seems
as though Beauvoir had consciously refrained from giving too much
prominence to some of her explorations, lest she be accused of
"stardom," or "vedettariat," an expression created around the 1968
student rebellion and which she quotes. Her newfound discretion is
another reason why this volume deserves attention and even close
scrutiny: besides, many essential ideas are discussed in it, some old,
some new or revived from earlier days, and the writer certainly has
much to offer to her readers willing to overlook the flaws.

Some of Beauvoir's essays written with a certain impulsiveness
and spontaneity, responding to urges of the day, such as, for example, *America Day by Day* and *La Longue Marche (The Long
March)*, may not stand up to the test of time. They did, however,
serve as "clearing houses"—that is, to try out ideas, depict land-
scapes, filter impressions garnered recently, and thus lead to a
clearer historical perspective or prepare ultimately for the writing of
more substantial works. Probably, the last volume of memoirs, *All*

Said and Done, fulfills a similar function. At any rate, it contains brilliant passages and also very dull ones.

XIX *A Statement of Intentions*

From the outset, in the Prologue, the tone of the writing is simple and straightforward. Simone de Beauvoir answers those critics who showed too much curiosity by another candid examination of her position. Ten years have passed since the preceding volume of memoirs, and she now wishes to look at her life once more, without, this time, following any strictly chronological order. "For me, she writes, life was an undertaking that had a clear direction. . . . But no public or private event has made any fundamental change in my position: I have not altered."[7] Just the same, the reader will note an increasing awareness of death, as in this quiet remark, neither over-emphasized nor underplayed: "[I feel that] I am slipping inevitably towards my grave . . ." (ii). As will be seen shortly, this premonition does not prevent Simone de Beauvoir from remaining at peace with her fate.

Questions of identity preoccupy the author who, from the start of the book, asks: "Why am I myself?" (1) while discussing the role of chance in her life: she does not believe that her life would have been essentially different if certain important encounters or events had turned out differently. Sooner or later, she might have met Sartre, she feels. Sooner or later, she would have made the acquaintance of other prominent writers and artists. Sooner or later, she would have chosen her career the way she did: "it is therefore reasonable for me to feel that I am myself contingent" (1).

As for her destiny, she feels satisfied with it and would not want it different in any way. Speaking of her serene childhood, the author remarks on how deeply early childhood experiences mark our lives. She muses on elements of her late friend Zaza's life that were brought to her attention only after she wrote her earlier memoirs and concludes: "For me, Zaza's murder [*sic*] by her environment, her milieu was an overwhelming, unforgettable experience. And then how grey and dismal and lonely my youth and adolescence would have been without Zaza! She was my only thoroughly happy connection with life outside of books . . . " (10). Simone de Beauvoir also redefines the deeper reasons for her loss of faith in the context of her position toward the class from which she herself had come, the middle class. She insists on the part played by the past in her life—in fact in all our lives—when she finds that in the crisis of faith, "it does not appear to me that I really made any free election—I followed the path that my earlier life pointed out for me so imperatively . . ." (12). But these decisions were made at the time for reasons perhaps not altogether in line with what a later analysis would yield.

More convincing are reflections on other aspects of her youth, as her assertion that her freedom "never took the form of a *decree* . . ." (12). And continuing with a statement that obviously corresponds to her later personality "I was never inert: I called out for life and welcomed it" (12)—and the typical elation over the progress of her emancipation—"the idea of earning my own living by work I liked filled me with delight: all the more so since my being a woman seemed to foredoom me to dependence" (12). In light of the forcefully stated concept of women's rights, it is indeed in order here to credit the memorialist with candor in her narrative of her own evolution, especially when what she faithfully recorded seemed to go against her convictions—at least in part.

The same openness is to be noted when the author evokes her own and her family's indifference to social matters: it explains the long delay in her eventual acceptance of intellectual responsibility in the betterment of the evils of society. In retrospect, Beauvoir credits her background with some of the more momentous decisions in her life: "My attitude during the Occupation was prescribed to me by my past—by my whole scale of values and my convictions" (24). At other moments, existentialist jargon causes formulations that appear exaggerated nonchalance, as this one, less offensive in English than in French, to be sure: "A writer writes from the basis of the being that he has made of himself, but writing is always a fresh act" (27).[8]

In the "enterprise" of writing, Simone looked for her bearings; she now feels that she always was faithful to her original design: "that of knowing and writing" (28). We may grant her that she has in fact been faithful to that goal, having shown the diligence and the patience of one who really wants to know before she writes—except perhaps on very minor points where she proved less scrupulous.[9] One of the weightier arguments for her way of writing is furnished when she finds that her own example strikingly shows how deeply an individual is endebted to childhood experiences. She continues:

"My life has been the fulfillment of a primary design and at the same time it has been the product and the expression of the world in which it developed. That is why in telling it, I have been able to speak of a great deal other than myself" (30). This would seem to be the nearest explanation of why innumerable readers have reacted to Simone de Beauvoir's published memoirs in such a strong way. More than an individual life, her testimony became the revelation of what millions of people had not spelled out to themselves: their dreams, their disillusions, their struggles, and their hopes.

The memorialist herself has insisted on her intention of giving more than a mere self-portrait: "I wanted to share in a perenniality in which I should be embodied, but above all I wanted my contemporaries to hear and understand me. It is my relationship with them—cooperation, struggle, dialogue—that has meant most to me throughout my life" (29).

XX *At Ease in Her Position*

Looking back on the years of her literary activity, in particular since she finished *Force of Circumstance*, Beauvoir does not feel she has aged any more. Between 1958 and 1962, she was aware of having "crossed a frontier," an expression she emphasizes by repeating it (30, 34). But while she was writing, time seemed to stand still, all the more intensely as people nearest to her are not "affected . . . by the scale of ages" (33). The only indication that ageing ceaselessly takes place is given by Beauvoir, who is "neither a slave to [her] past nor haunted by it" (32): a certain "shrinking of the future is taking place" (34)—the author attributes the formula to Michel Leiris. She notes, taking stock of her work: "I . . . am aware of my own finity. Even if it is increased by two or three books, the body of my literary work will remain what it is" (34). Taken together with similar statements by the author, this sober summing up shows a writer interested in what she is doing without being blinded by vanity. Her work, to her, counts, and she is neither bashful nor arrogant about it.

Simone realizes that she was fortunate in many respects: "I have not shared in the lot of the vast majority of mankind—exploitation, repression, extreme poverty. I am privileged" (39). This realization of privilege goes together with a major change in her outlook; her new attitude toward death: "I no longer feel the haunting anxiety of death that was so strong in my youth. I have given up rebelling against it. . . . My indignation is now directed only against evils stirred up by men" (40). This relative serenity does not mean indifference. "Yet, the idea of my end is with me," writes Beauvoir; "the taste of the void is deep within me" (40).

This changed attitude toward death goes together, also, with a sense of urgency in matters of professional interest. Writing remains the great concern of her life, the memorialist states at the beginning of the second chapter. Reviewing a number of her more recent books, she endeavors to defend them against misinterpretations which, according to her, have vitiated the understanding of some of them. "Above all, I try to understand my own period," she declares elsewhere (141).

Traveling proved to be the most enduring and the most durably rewarding of her activities. Sartre and she grew into the habit of spending summers, every year, in Rome, where they felt comfortably installed to work and live. In Rome, she avidly reads novels, sociological and anthropological treatises, psychological abstracts, and many more essays on a great variety of subjects. Reading without a purpose, too, gives her a feeling of pleasure, and she enjoys the relaxing quality of detective stories.

Her comments on her readings are often very detailed; she dwells on why and how she enjoys certain books or why and for what specific reason she is more critically inclined toward others. The *Times Literary Supplement* accuses her of merely summarizing her readings. Yet, on the contrary, from all those books she devours, like a typical "bibliophage" or "book-swallower" (140).[10] Simone de Beauvoir is extracting the very substance which enables her to discuss the value of individual books.

XXI *Whatever Became of Those Old Associates?*

"What shows me the number of my years most decisively is the complete change that has come about in my scale of ages. This scale does not affect those who are close to me" (33). While Proust tells us how, one day, the grandmother he knew was replaced by a very old woman, Simone de Beauvoir feels that people close to her don't change. Strangers or remote acquaintances of course do. Thinking back on her past, the memorialist evokes old friendships and at the same time marvels at the ease with which she struck up new ones even at what she calls an advanced age, as in the case of Violette Leduc, whom she met when both were well beyond middle age.

Some of the evocations are moving and graceful. Others leave an embarrassing impression: strung together, one after the other, the mostly poignant stories of friendships and the almost inevitable demise of many of the writer's friends cause the awful feeling of having to listen to a chatting, tireless gossip. The narrator herself seems to be the only stable point in a world out of joint; the deterioration in her several friends is almost fateful: does she feel they were all doomed because they were her friends? Or was the writer simply fascinated by their stories because of their weird, often morbid qualities? However that may be, it is strange to read such an extraordinary collection of hard luck stories, all of them about people who once were close to the author.

The malaise the reader may experience must be credited to the authenticity of the stories. If they all were fiction, we would not bat an eyelash. But while reading how the beautiful Camille*, who in her prime brought light into the lives of Dullin and Sartre, was to decline so pathetically and to die miserably, we may feel like a person who entered a room, unaware that something of a very private nature was going on there, and is unable to leave discreetly. The same uneasy feeling prevails throughout the account of the life of another of Simone's close friends, Lise. The individual had received too precise a treatment for the reader to dismiss her from memory as a mere character in a literary framework. Many more of the author's close associates were seen through the prism of the memorialist's testimony—a view far from flattering for most of them.

The uneasy impression does not necessarily linger long enough to spoil the reader's pleasure in encountering some of Simone de Beauvoir's new friends, even though these, too, often eventually decline virtually before our eyes. The author shows herself an artist in friendship; the pages on friendship speak in the plain language of affection, of interests shared and causes pursued in common. Besides people in Paris or simply fellow writers or journalists, Beauvoir befriended others whom she encountered in various parts of the world. Thus, her Japanese interpreter, Tomiko, became a good friend, and so did the Russian interpreter, Lena, who traveled a good deal with her and Sartre. The author shows how all her friends obviously enrich her life. Giving unstintingly of herself to her friends, she knows she can expect advice and help from them as well as comfort in days of need or crisis.

XXII   A Bridge between Generations

Her friends are complementing her intellectual work, keeping
her from living only in books. She now feels secure in her political
and social orientation and capable of steering a clear course:

So I still go on cultivating my mind. Am I more informed than I used to be
or less? I never stop learning, but knowledge grows so fast that at the same
time my ignorance increases. And my memory lets a great deal of learning I
had stored up leak away. It was above all between the ages of twenty-five
and fifty that I lost so much—almost everything I knew of mathematics,
Latin and Greek. I remember only the broad outlines of the systems of
philosophy that I studied in former days and I have not read the books
devoted to them these last twenty years. . . . On the whole I see where I
stand in the world more clearly than when I was forty. (208)

Greater ease in her relationship to the world at large may in part
derive from the way Simone had cultivated her taste in music and
learned to know and like modern music. She also deepened her
understanding of painting and, in general, of artists and their work.
She had always had a keen interest in the theatre. Once more we
see a thinker of robust intellectual appetites more and more at
unison with her times. That, probably, is one of the reasons why
Simone de Beauvoir, nearing seventy, is attuned to young people
better than ever before. They acclaim her on many scores, and yet,
at the same time, she felt they were opposed to knowledge and to
learning.

Hence a change in her intellectual direction:

I am addressing myself to all men. But I reach only a limited audience. At
the present time many of the young whom I should particularly like to
reach, look upon reading as pointless. So I no longer see writing as a
privileged means of communication. And yet I have carried this book on to
the end and no doubt I shall write others: I may indeed challenge the worth
of the writer that I am, but I cannot tear myself from that writer's personality. I cannot toss my past overboard and deny everything I have
loved. . . . (209)

The realization of the limits to communication was a hard one to
come by; no doubt the writer felt hurt by the refusal of young people
to go to the trouble of reading, not just her books but any books. As
she had leaned on books and learning all her life and had cherished

the acquisition of knowledge above all else, it came as a shock to her that today's generation has different ideas and wants different things from life. But, true to her determination to understand her own period, Beauvoir is trying to keep in touch with the live forces among the young people. The makeup of her mind helps her in that respect, since she always was eager to learn from foreign nations or from representatives of other classes. The young now appear to her, to a degree, like another nation to acquaint herself with, to explore, and to conquer. Dynamic and patient, full of the desire to understand, more than to persuade, she is bound to succeed in reaching today's youth.

XXIII *Travel Abroad*—Travel through Life

If the fourth volume of memoirs *(All Said and Done)* contains less of an account of actual evolution in Beauvoir, it nevertheless shows the writer adjusting to some of the major concerns of her life. Her fear of death, as we have seen, is significantly diminished. Her certainty of holding the truth, always moderated by common sense, yields to the desire of being understood. Added to these changes in her perception of the world is a growing need for reconciling the experience gathered with the uncertainty of the future. "It is the memory of the past," she writes, "and the promise of the future that most surely give the living person the illusion of catching up with his being. . . . I am both memory and expectation, intensely aware of what is leaving me and of what is just about to come" (213).

One way of enriching her life had always been travel to unknown countries. For political reasons, but also for her own enjoyment, Beauvoir continues to see new places. In France, where she had restricted her trips during the Algerian War, she again found many beautiful and memorable sights. Her pleasure was enhanced, she reports, through her ability to "name" the monuments of the past.

Accounts of her various trips through the Soviet Union are rather monotonous. The descriptions are too long, too impersonal; too little of each place is shown. Notations of people, in general, are more detailed and convey an impression of friendliness everywhere in the USSR. The enormous Soviet bureaucracy emerges through the pages of these travel notes, mostly anonymous, though we are allowed to approach a few personalities from close range. Among the most vividly described scenes are the unending drinking bouts with endless obligatory toasts by Sartre in response to toasts to him. No wonder both Sartre and Beauvoir came to dread such trials by vodka.

The twin trips to Egypt and Israel, in 1967, are told in a strikingly contrasting way. While during the Egyptian tour there are glowing tributes to the friendliness of the people—the sole exception is the politically "rehearsed" Gaza trip and the embarrassingly crude propaganda there—and the beauty of the land with its towering monuments is extolled, the trip to Israel is narrated in a tone so different as to suggest a strong bias against that country. This is striking indeed, as Beauvoir at all times has maintained an attitude of definite support for Israel, even though she has expressed her sympathy and understanding for Arab aspirations in general and especially for the Palestinian refugees.

In a way, this evolution also mirrors Beauvoir's and Sartre's own perplexities when confronting the problem of Marxism. Both writers dreamed of a socialist society, without the rigors of Bolshevik bureaucracy and dogmatism. Both are, naturally, disillusioned when actual experiments with socialism show the drift toward more dogmatic interpretations of socialism.

XXIV *The Activist*

Political disappointments could not long dampen the memorialist's enthusiasm for basic ideals. Exploring the globe gives her a feeling of mastery, of exhilaration unparalleled by other pursuits. "Exploring this planet I live upon still gives me as much pleasure as it ever did; and in this respect time has given me as much as it has taken away—perhaps more indeed" (250). Slowing down on other activities, becoming if not more thrifty with her time, at least more discriminating in accepting or refusing obligations, Simone de Beauvoir has for the first time started to limit her participation in political causes.

It is therefore all the more significant to study the causes which she and Sartre continued to support over the last six to eight years when health problems and simple fatigue have made both writers conscious of their physical "contingence". When the 1968 student uprising occurred, both writers went to investigate the demands made by the students. They showed their interest in, indeed their solidarity with, the strikers. Simone de Beauvoir records the spread of student demands over the whole world and examines the situation in various countries where these demands met with stiff opposition.

The memorialist's account of the student revolt in 1968 rings true, especially as Beauvoir had no compunction about showing her own inadequacies: when an insistant professor at the Sorbonne arranged for a confrontation between Beauvoir and the students, and a young woman gave her a snippy reply, the writer sensed she was in a false position and recognized it openly.

Even more direct is the account of the incident around *La Cause du Peuple*: this passage in her memoirs may be material too raw to make a "good" book. It does, however, make for a book true to life as a document of our time.

The memoirs have reviewed her whole life. She has recorded her reactions as an individual to lessened ability in, and less enjoyment of, certain things. Her observations are as vivid as ever. Her interests seem undiminished. Her energy is still remarkable, even though she says she is reducing some of her many activities. Now as before, she enjoys reading, she states, and music remains one of her greatest pleasures; usually, she enjoys listening to it in her own home rather than in a concert hall. Her mind appears unimpaired by age, and the various handicaps or frailties that come with age are noted by her, not without humor, rather uncomplainingly. While Sartre, owing to almost total blindness, is no longer able to read or write, Beauvoir helps him on many levels. She is robust and full of vigor, living her days fully and continuing her work at her own pace.

XXV   *The Militant Feminist*

As a pioneer of the women's movement, Simone de Beauvoir has contributed immeasurably to the progress and the strengthening of women's conscience and emancipation. No wonder she was solicited by various feminist organizations who wanted her help in advancing their cause. Her response has almost always been entirely positive, with perhaps a more cautionary attitude over the years when such demands became more and more numerous. Fundamentally, of course, there could never be any question on whether Simone de Beauvoir would support bona fide feminists. It became a matter of ability: would she be able to address another congress, to write yet another manifesto, to draft more petitions?

In her account of women's activist movements, in *All Said and
Done*, the author gives an overview of what has been achieved and
what remains to be done. In so doing, she gives, along with many
accurate explanations, a few that are counter to fact. After showing
herself at present more committed to women's liberation, she notes
the titles of several books by American feminist activists; some of
these titles are erroneous, because the memorialist retranslated
them from French into English without verifying them. Correctly,
the author analyzes the position of women in various groups and
movements, stating: "even in the most authentically revolutionary
groups, women are only given the most unpleasant tasks, and all the
leaders are male" (454). But immediately after this vigorous statement, the author lapses, attributing a completely wrong origin to
the women's movement in the United States: "In their tactics and
their forms of action, the feminists of today have been influenced, in
the United States, by the hippies, the yippies and above all by the
Black Panthers" (455). The birth of the women's movement predates
those groups, and the movement has remained largely unaffected by
their extremism.

On the positive side, it must be remembered that Beauvoir
avoids the crude exaggerations of certain feminists who refuse to
acknowledge any male contribution whatsoever to culture or
technology (458–59). Her point of view is flexible, but she never
wavers on matters of fairness or basic principle. She found fulfillment in her own struggle for women's rights and declares that she is
determined to continue to participate in that fight.

Finally and most emphatically, Simone de Beauvoir restates her
fundamentally agnostic view of life. Faced with frequent laments by
some correspondents who deplored her loss of faith, she finds a calm
and fairly unaggressive way of affirming her position on religious
scores. Inevitably, the next question that one would ask her is, How
does she make up for the lack of faith? Her answer is simple and
direct: neither a blind optimist, nor an out-and-out pessimist, she
recalls her love of life, her "delight in happiness," but also her active
stance against evils in society. The volume ends without a formal
conclusion—but that is a conclusion in itself:

My natural bent certainly does not lead me to suppose that the worst is
always inevitable. Yet I am committed to looking reality in the face and to
speaking without pretence. . . . To fight unhappiness one must first expose

it, which means that one must dispel the mystifications behind which it is hidden. . . . It is because I reject lies and running away that I am accused of pessimism; but this rejection implies hope—the hope that truth may be of use. And this is a more optimistic attitude than the choice of indifference, ignorance or sham. (462–63)

All Said and Done, then, is not nearly as disabused, as bland or pallid as its title or even some of the initial statements by the author would indicate. On balance, Beauvoir found life worth living, having paid the penalty of ageing and of losing some of her illusions, but not her basic faith in man. With some losses, some pains, and many disappointments, to be sure, she also noted the sense of mastery over life, of usefulness in bringing hope to many readers, of elation in seeing young people acclaim her efforts and encourage her to continue her work. A woman who found fulfillment in being a writer does not need to conceal her weaknesses and blemishes. That is why even a somewhat uneven volume of memoirs by Simone de Beauvoir deserves attention and respect and adds to her merit.

CHAPTER 4

The Essays

I A Brief Definition of Existentialism

SIMONE de Beauvoir's thinking and writing was done in close
cooperation with Sartre's and proceeds from existentialist
premises; it therefore seems fitting to attempt a concise definition of
Sartrean existentialism, all the more so as, particularly in the United
States, it has spawned all sorts of confused, mostly erroneous, notions. As this study is not primarily concerned with philosophy, a
mere working formula of existentialism may suffice.

A recent *History of French Literature* affords us the most precise
wording to characterize the movement: "Philosophical trends born
from phenomenology, upsetting the postulates of classical philosophy, assert the primacy of existence over essence in man; to
use Sartre's formulation, they claim that 'primarily man *is*, and only
after that is he this or that.' Such an attitude naturally implies a new
set of answers to the manifold interrogations that mark the history of
thought . . ."[1]

While this statement applies to all types of existentialism, Christian existentialism, mainly voiced by Gabriel Marcel and Nicholas
Berdyaev, is distinct from the more influential atheist strain, the
only one to be discussed here. Camus, of course, has often been
considered close to existentialism, but he was careful to insist on his
autonomy; he never belonged to the existentialist group.

Man's loneliness is one of the fundamental themes of Sartre's
brand of existentialism: no help is to be expected from any god
whatsoever since no being could exist prior to its own existence.
Consequently, man is abandoned, obliged to conquer his own freedom—"condemned to be free," as Sartre has it in *Being and Nothingness*. Thence it follows that man is compelled to choose an
essence, a choice from which he has no chance of escaping. Free-

106

dom consists in choosing, but that does not mean freedom not to choose: "Not to choose means indeed to choose not to choose."[2] Hence the absurdity of freedom, which creates our responsibility in the eyes of the world.

What is the nature of our relationship with the world? For phenomenological existentialism, the raw given fact *(l'en soi)* "can only accede to significance by my personal action: it thereby becomes a 'pour moi' that is variable according to the plan of each conscience. Thus, the revelation of the object is also revelation of man. . . . "[3] The thing in itself, then, becomes significant through our making it ours. Responsibility is one aspect of the existentialist's life; freedom is its complement.

The freedom here discussed is illustrated by Sartre in his play *The Flies*, where freedom literally breaks out, marking man's victory over the gods, who held men under their heel only as long as men did not realize that they were meant to be free. "I *am* my freedom," says Orestes in *The Flies*, thereby shaking off the yoke of prejudice and obscurantism. All men, Sartre implies, must accept their freedom, thus also accepting responsibility. Only when man combines freedom with responsibility can he achieve his independence and carry out his mission.

Existentialism is "not a closed chapel but a mood," according to Henri Peyre,[4] an opinion shared by Germaine Brée in her vigorous thumbnail sketch of existentialism. This mood is dominant in most of Sartre's fiction and plays, as well as in Simone de Beauvoir's novels, where the notion of "bad faith" plays a seminal role. Existentialism places great stress on the value of what is authentic. Conversely, every act lacking authenticity is tinged with corruption. "Bad faith" is suspected whenever a character is not spontaneous or forthright. The evil of inauthenticity was fought by existentialist writers in every walk of life, much as existentialism was not confined to philosophy but invaded literature, the social sciences, and everyday life. No wonder that in the protracted controversy that ensued, Sartre was taken to task for alleged moral turpitude (on grounds that now, thirty years later, would evoke an indulgent smile), and "existentialist" became a term of abuse.

Sartre's existentialism was an outgrowth of phenomenological preoccupations in the wake of studies of Kierkegaard and his pessimism; of Hegel (and historical materialism) some of whose theories led to Marxism; of Husserl and phenomenology proper; and of

Heidegger, who led the way for a time in detaching his brand of existentialist philosophy from religion. Sartre's type of existentialism shows "anguish linked to freedom," as Jean Bruneau put it.[5] This Sartrean existentialism "severs our links with the past; it depicts us as perpetually making a choice which projects us into the future, and divorces human reality from material reality," in Peyre's words.[6]

Germaine Brée reminds us that the term "existentialism" became popular in Paris at the time of the Liberation. More than a philosophical system, she states, it is, rather, a philosophical attitude:

The originality of French existentialism as it appeared in the forties was that it succeeded in integrating the emotional mood of the moment with the intellectual structures of existentialist philosophy. Had Sartre . . . and Simone de Beauvoir not shared the latent anxieties of their contemporaries, and had they failed to express them in their fictional worlds, existentialism might never have been familiar to any but the professional philosophers. However, the fictional worlds of these writers proved all the more challenging because they formulated and attempted to answer coherently the problems which were implicit in the mood of the time.[7]

Thus existentialism became, for all practical purposes, a household word, encompassing too vast an array of ideas and tendencies for any one individual, let alone any group, to live by. But precisely living by the tenets of existentialism, one way or another, had become the watchword. While the word had taken on negative connotations in the eyes of conservative and reactionary Frenchmen, it meant positive values for many others. An existentialist was a person believing in his or her own freedom. This freedom implied responsibility and human solidarity. In the Voltairean sense, a pessimistic, therefore activist, view of the world was the earmark of much of existentialist moral philosophy. "The other," in the view of the existentialist, became the necessary partner, and life had to be authentic—that is, free from lies and pretense.

It goes without saying that the actual concepts of existentialism were far less shallow and superficial. The movement itself did not fall out of a blue sky but owed much of its substance to the humanistic tradition, even though it had seemed fashionable to frown on humanism. Through its literary embodiments, existentialism appears as an attempt to make life more livable at a time of depressing experiences of war and destruction. Existentialist pessimism, being free of delusions with regard to man's possibilities, actually helped man out of seemingly hopeless situations by obliging him to use his resourcefulness, unaided by metaphysical forces. Contrary to its detractors' claims, none of its tenets dictated amoral or immoral behavior. Whatever immoral acts were committed within the framework of existentialism cannot be blamed on the movement itself, which never condoned eccentricity.

More revealing than these observations on the more or less acceptable nature of existentialism are the findings one cannot help making when reading the texts of existentialist writers. It becomes immediately clear that certainly theirs is not a literature of despair or of the graveyard. It is a testimony to life, with its ups and downs, where nothing need be concealed from an enlightened reader. Whatever shocked certain prudish readers is by far less offensive than the average accepted reading fare of the 1950s and 1960s, to say nothing of the much more explicit literature of the seventies. That is not to say that fig leaves abounded in existentialist writing, but simply that it did not occur to any existentialist author to belabor erotic episodes. Rather, existentialists were explicit about physiological processes and outspoken about subjective feelings and perceptions. Thus, Sartre's Roquentin voices his disgust vehemently, and Simone de Beauvoir's characters follow their own propensities, without indulging in anything even remotely obscene. That is why, today, we may wonder about the violently antiexistentialist diatribes of quite a few critics of the 1940s and 1950s.

There may never be a consensus on what existentialism is or is not, as Henri Peyre wrote, nor "as to what 'existence,' 'nothingness,' 'the absurd,' 'a project,' or our moral duty as discovered by our own derelict self and still valid for other men, may signify."[8] Some saw it, especially during the years 1945–1955, as a philosophy of decadence. Peyre uses a cogent and lively diagnosis when he reminds us that "the originality and the force of French existentialism is that it did not stay enclosed in university seminars of philosophy and wrapped in abstruse language."[9] It is "literature as philosophy," a formula used by Everett Knight, and pervades life in many forms.

Peyre goes on to show that the importance of a movement, ideological, aesthetic, and even political, "cannot be measured clearly by the number of persons who present themselves as belonging to it, but by the quality of their sensibility and the power of their ideas. . . ." In the same vein, using the example of Surrealism, Peyre shows that many artists, in and outside France, were influenced by it and goes on to demonstrate similar trends in existentialism:

There may . . . never have been more than sixty existentialists, or sixty surrealists; nevertheless those movements constituted the marching wing of French literature for several decades. None rivalled them in importance. . . . The years 1940–1965 may well be labeled, in future histories of taste, the existentialist era. Nor does it seem of much consequence to debate at length who was, or was not, a genuine existentialist, or an authentic surrealist, or a true romantic. Existentialism never constituted a chapel, or a school, from which a heretic or an unruly child is expelled: it is a mood.[10]

II   L'Existentialisme et la Sagesse des Nations *(1948)*

One of the best and clearest answers to questions on the nature of existentialism is given by Simone de Beauvoir in a volume of essays published in 1948. In her preface, the author states: "These days, whenever existentialism is attacked, ordinarily it is not because another well-defined doctrine is preferred over it but rather because philosophy in general is denied any value. . . ."[11] This may or may not be true. What is debatable is another view of opposing echoes: "one cannot blame existentialist aesthetics in the name of absolute principles, as these do not exist, because literature is what man makes it to be" (10). If one grants that literature is manmade art, aesthetics follow, and cannot be divorced from the work of art.

More valid and more specifically helpful is a declaration of purpose that focuses on the provable contribution of existentialism: "these essays do not seek to define, once more, what existentialism is," writes Beauvoir; "they try to defend it against the reproach of being frivolous and gratuitous which, frivolously and gratuitously, has been directed, ever since Socrates, against any organized thought. In truth, there is no divorce between philosophy and life" (12). That unity of life and philosophy is one of the most vigorous assertions made by writers in the existentialist camp. It is borne out, increasingly, through their choice of social and political commitment, which, in turn, alienates those critics who frown on any association of life and art.

In the first essay, Beauvoir summarizes some of the militant statements about the movement that were provoked by adverse criticism:

Few people actually know this philosophy which has been rather randomly baptized existentialism. Many people attack it. What it is being reproached for, among other things, is that it is offering man an image of himself and of his condition that is apt to make him despair. Existentialism, it is claimed, does not recognize man's greatness and chooses to depict only his misery. According to a newly coined phrase, existentialism is accused of 'miserabilism'; it is, its critics contend, a doctrine negating friendship, brotherhood, and all manifestations of love; it confines the individual in a selfish kind of loneliness, retrenching him from the real world and condemning him to remain isolated in his pure subjectivity; for existentialism is said to refuse any objective justification in human endeavors, as well as values cherished by man and the goals he pursues. . . . (13)

The case thus forcefully—and none too fairly—stated, the author continues her plea for greater understanding. She tries to dispel what she calls misrepresentations of the movement, relying on the old military principle that attack is the best defense:

The very first reproach addressed to existentialism is that it is [they claim] a coherent and organized system, a philosophical attitude requiring to be adopted integrally. Taking a too precisely defined view of the world, those critics would be afraid to burden themselves with too weighty responsibilities. . . . For men above all else fear responsibilities; they don't like to take risks; they are so deadly afraid of committing or engaging their freedom that they prefer denying that very freedom. That is the deepest reason of their repugnance toward a doctrine placing that freedom in the forefront. (38)

The heavy stress on responsibility and solidarity might be discounted as a merely polemical trait. Yet existentialism manages to convey its message of activism and trust in man, with all individual reservations about character and personality, and the movement gathers force through resilient and forceful arguments put forth by its defenders. Simone de Beauvoir more concretely states her belief thus: "What existentialism wishes to accomplish is avoiding for man the disappointments and sulking moroseness which a certain cult of false idols brings with it; existentialism wants to teach man how to

be authentically a man. Such a philosophy is capable of boldly refusing the shallow comfort of lies and of resignation. Existentialism
ultimately has confidence in man" (52–53).

In defining attitudes of existentialist writers, Beauvoir finds
herself in agreement with some of the finest minds outside the
movement itself, with writers affirming humanistic values. One
such statement recalls the forceful defense of man and refusal of
hair-splitting trickery illustrated by Vercors in *Les Yeux et la
Lumière* (1947), and again in *Plus ou moins Homme* (1950) where the
same point was made in closely similar terms. She writes: "if you
treat man as a means, that is violating man, it is contradicting that
idea of his absolute value which is the only one idea permitting our
actions to be fully well-founded. (Even though I killed but one man
in order to save millions, there would be a shocking scandal erupt-
ing on my account in this world, a scandal that no success could
compensate for . . .)" (98).

No wonder Simone de Beauvoir is finding herself in unison with
some of her contemporary humanists: her thought eventually
meets—in this essay—one of her models, if an unconscious one—
Pascal. For some of her reasoning sounds like a perfect pastiche of
the *Pensées,* especially where Pascal deals with man's smallness as
compared to the infinite universe and with man's greatness as compared to the infinitely small:

Therefore, let man lose his hope of taking refuge in his inner purity just as
much as of losing himself in a foreign object; temporal dispersion, separation of consciences do not permit him to dream of definitive reconciliation
with himself; he feels torn asunder, and that is his ransom for being present
in this world, for his transcendance and his freedom. If he tries to flee, the
only thing he will accomplish is losing himself; he does nothing, or else what
he does amounts to nothing. He must give up every hope of ever knowing
rest, he must accept his freedom. Only at that price does he become capable of truly overcoming the given situation, which is the genuine ethics, and
of founding in truth the object in which he transcends himself, which is the
only valid policy. At that price, his action is concretely inscribed in the
world, and the world where he acts is a world endowed with a meaning, a
human world. (100)

While this adjuration may not be terribly original in its wording,
it reiterates some of the fundamental tenets of existentialism, and it
does not lack in vigor or clarity. Such was Simone de Beauvoir's

orientation at that time; she was feeling the need and the mission to defend a movement of which she had become an integral part. All essays in this volume had been published first in *Les Temps Modernes*. But by contrast with the first, from which these ample quotations were chosen, the others address more current problems: II—"Moral idealism and political realism," seen in the context of the political spectrum of the day, is self-contained. III—"Literature and metaphysics" treats a specific problem, pleading for acceptance of metaphysical novels. IV—"An eye for an eye" is perhaps the most enduring of these later essays. It deals with the trials of collaborationists after the Liberation.

Viewing her essays after about twenty years, when she wrote her memoirs, the author is struck by what she calls "the idealism which heavily taints those essays."[12] Without altogether condemning them, or reneging, she seems to regret the intensity of her desire to convince in writing them.

III   *Other Philosophical and Literary Essays; Travelogues*

Much the same is true of most of her other philosophical essays: *Pyrrhus et Cinéas* (1944) endeavors to confront the problem of absurdity. It again demonstrates the author's constant concern with the "other." The essay is a robust attempt at expressing philosophical thought in plain language. *Pour une Morale de l'Ambiguité (The Ethics of Ambiguity,* 1947) has some merit, although twenty years after she wrote it, Beauvoir criticized it, thinking that its weak points overshadowed its strong ones.

L'Amérique au jour le jour (America Day by Day, 1947) is a subjective view of some portions of American culture and life. While no Toqueville, the twentieth century traveler showed a fair understanding of most essential aspects of what seemed to her a disconcerting country. *La longue Marche (The Long March,* 1957), despite its flaws, is a human document likely to enrich our knowledge of China. Witnessing the tumultuous life of Chinese cities, or pondering wisdom of China's past, Beauvoir communicated her passionate desire to serve as a mediator between East and West.

Privilèges (1955) combines an excellent literary essay on the Marquis de Sade with reflections on rightist thought of the postwar period in France and a polemical piece, "Merleau-Ponty and pseudo-Sartrism." All of these had at some time been published in Sartre's monthly, *Les Temps Modernes*. These essays, while written on topical themes, give an excellent illustration of the scope of Simone de Beauvoir's interests, her knowledge and insight in various intellectual domains, and the originality of her thought. Space limitations are the only reason for the omission of these significant writings from the present study. A more detailed treatment of these subjects is to be published separately.

IV   Le Deuxième Sexe (1949) The Second Sex

A definition of this book might be easily attempted by stating first what it is not. It is definitely not a weighty scientific treatise written pedantically and without human warmth. Neither is it sheer polemic, a cheap and superficial tract launched exclusively in defense of women's rights. It may come close to offering itself as a target on most of these scores, yet there is more substance to Simone de Beauvoir's work than in any one of the supposed guises that detractors found it convenient to suspect.

While the author documents herself scrupulously, going to the sources of whatever field she investigates, quoting with precision, using materials not readily available in their wide scope and enormous variety of specialties, she is not always cautious nor skilled enough to avoid pitfalls through some hasty oversimplifications. Her enemies have claimed that such "bloopers" annul the scientific impact of her book on its readership. These overstatements show the lack of good faith, the bias of critics who would not be so severe if the amateur sociologist were not so right in the substance of her findings. As it stands, The Second Sex is an honest attempt by a thinker of high integrity at recording why women had to struggle so long and hard to gain even the limited recognition of their place in society that has been achieved to date.

Simone de Beauvoir did not set out to "free women." Her aim was far more modest: by explaining historically, biologically, psychologically, sociologically, and philosophically what women's condition has been through the ages, she has eventually equipped the combative champions of women's rights in our day with the weapons to be used in the continued fight for equality and justice, as it turned out not only for women but for all human beings treated unfairly. For the last few years, Beauvoir has herself claimed a place in that battle and has spoken out more pointedly even than in The Second Sex on a number of burning issues such as abortion. In so doing, she has added another dimension to her personality.

More recent editions of *The Second Sex* have corrected a number of errors, but the author's view that her book, now thirty years old, should be regarded as a moment in the history of women's liberation, not as the definitive study, stands unaltered. Added to this is the fact that Beauvoir's fight against social injustice continues, witness the substantial study of ageing which is the subject of the second part of this chapter.

By its very nature, *The Second Sex* affords mankind a revealing insight into one of the more shameful sins of omission, the long overdue recognition of the rights of women. Reading its often arid prose, one discovers that the trained philosopher went systematically about her task of marshaling the impressive amount of materials she pored over, using a rigorous set of standards that enabled her to give a rational account of the fate of one-half of the human race. While she never completely shunned the aggressive, polemical tone of the earnest fighter for progress and fairness for women, she obviously was bent on as objective a course to steer as her strong indignation would allow her to muster. The failings of the book— and there are a number of these—must be ascribed not so much to partisanship, which the author had no intention of concealing, as to her overeager incorporation of matters not necessarily germane to all phases of her generally apt demonstration.

V *The Setting of the Task*

Simone de Beauvoir starts out in her Introduction by giving a historical exposé of the condition of women through the ages. She takes emphatic care to show the analogous situation of all minorities—Jews, blacks, and women—stipulating at once that women are not actually a minority, numerically. Admittedly, the essayist hesitated for a long time before embarking on the writing of *The Second Sex*. "Are there indeed any women?" is a highly classical, seventeenth century way of posing the problem. To refuse the notions of the "eternal feminine," of the "black soul," or of a "Jewish character disposition" is not denying, according to the writer of the essay, that today there are Jews, blacks, and women. Such a negation, for those concerned, does not represent a sort of liberation but inauthentic flight from reality.

Examining the idea of "the other," the author sees woman determining her own position and distinguishing herself in relationship to man, but man does not differentiate himself from woman. She is what is inessential, facing the essential. He is subject and an absolute, whereas she is the other. Such a demonstration, while explicitly leaning on conventional usage, sounds like the caricature of society, and yet, what else does woman face if not denial of her rights?

Simone de Beauvoir acknowledges that women cannot expect a definitive victory over their adversaries, and that is how they differ from other long-dominated groups. For, the essayist explains, no cleavage of society by sexes is possible. That is what fundamentally characterizes woman: she is the other amidst a totality both of whose terms are necessary to each other. Scanning the male writers who speak of women, the essayist singles out the most clear-cut cases of male disdain for women, such as the medieval poet, Jean de Meung, and the twentieth century writer, Henry de Montherlant; Montherlant's problems were, according to her, that he could show superiority only to women, feeling insecure in his own position. Montaigne, she writes, was fairer, without actually championing women's rights. Diderot was the first one to establish for all to see that, like man, woman is a human being.

It was almost inevitable that, having devoted a considerable part of her literary and philosophical work to existentialism, Beauvoir should place herself in the existentialist perspective in writing this book:

those who are condemned to stagnation are often pronounced happy on the pretext that happiness consists in being at rest. This notion we reject, for our perspective is that of existentialist ethics. Every subject plays his part as such specifically through exploits or projects that serve as a mode of transcendence; he achieves liberty only through a continual reaching out toward other liberties. There is no justification for present existence other than its expansion into an indefinitely open future. Every time transcendence falls back into immanence, stagnation, there is a degradation of existence into the *en-soi*, the brutish life of subjection to given conditions—and of liberty into constraint and contingence. . . . [13]

VI *The Components of Woman's Destiny*

The first chapter of the first part of the essay "Destiny" deals with biological facts. Reviewing the whole of the female species in most members of the animal kingdom, the author uses heavy artillery in an aggressively defensive onslaught on male neglect of the feminine factor in civilization. The various stages of her demonstration are unexceptionable. Thus, she finds that "the division of species into male and female individuals is simply an irreducible fact of observation" (6).

Examining female physiological phenomena from menstruation to conception and childbirth, Beauvoir traces the subjection of women in part to age-old superstitions relating to man's distrust of the feminine mystery. The myth of feminine impurity, the various prejudices regarding female intellectual capacities were invalidated by the findings that, substantially, brain activities and abilities are equal in both sexes; the vital statistics all speak for equality between the sexes. The statistics originally used by the author seem out of date with regard to mortality and longevity where thirty years of research play an important role, changing facts that were used by the essayist to support her theory, such as the one saying that "on an average, women live as long as men"; this particular one was revised, in subsequent editions, to read: "on an average, women live as long as men, or longer" (32).

The chapter closes on a defiant note. Insisting that the lengthy elaboration on physical elements in woman's condition was necessary because those are some of the keys enabling us to understand women, the writer emphatically refuses, in the name of all women, to accept the idea that for women, physical given facts constitute a fixed destiny. These facts, she writes, do not suffice to define a hierarchy of the sexes. They fail to explain why woman is "the other." They do not condemn her to accept forever this subordinate role.

The psychoanalytical point of view is the focus of the second chapter. Granting Freud the merit of having established certain basic sexual phenomena, Simone de Beauvoir underscores Freud's failings in explaining equality in sexual matters adequately and consistently. She finds that sexuality is only one aspect of the human being, and she combats confinement to just this one aspect. The essayist raises the matter in the context of Freudian and Adlerian synthesis—a synthesis that she envisages as possible—of what is "normal." " . . . among psychoanalysts in particular . . . man is defined as a human being and woman as a female," according to Donaldson, quoted by the essayist (51). "For us," she states, in a sort of credo, "woman is defined as a human being in quest of values in a world of values, a world of which it is indispensable to know the economic and social structure" (52).

Chapter three deals with the point of view of historical materialism. In a vast panorama going from cave man to push-button civilization, we are introduced to Beauvoir's philosophy of history, a philosophy closely akin, at times, to Jean-Jacques Rousseau's. Indeed, the origins of society are described in strictly Rousseauist terms. Before the invention of tools, woman was man's equal in all labors of the field. From the idyllic view of primitive woman, it takes only one step to the utopia of woman's future. Although Beauvoir is using rhetorical caution in speaking of Soviet propaganda relating to the future of women, stylistically at least the essayist seems to endorse the dream of a perfect society:

It is the resistance of the ancient capitalist paternalism that in most countries prevents the concrete realization of equality; it will be realized on the day when this resistance is broken, as is the fact already in the Soviet Union, according to Soviet propaganda. And when the socialist society is established throughout the world, there will no longer be men and women, but only workers on a footing of equality" (55).

After reminding us that August Bebel, toward the end of the nineteenth century, had called both woman and the proletarian the oppressed, Beauvoir accuses Engels of blurring the issues by limiting himself to declaring that a socialist community will abolish the family, which she correctly calls a rather abstract solution. To take full cognizance of the situation of women, says the essayist, one must go beyond historical materialism, which sees in man and woman only economic entities.

VII *Woman's Lot—Not a Fair Share*

With all its systematic effort at marshaling facts, statistics, and opinions, *The Second Sex* nevertheless remains a rather unsystematic plea for the obvious. From all the impressively garnered materials, it becomes crystal clear that man has not given woman a fair share of their respective places in society. Written thirty years ago, the book reflects truths as they were known then, and of course, recent decades have confirmed her findings on practically every score. What is amazing is not the relatively mild passion Beauvoir displays in proffering her accusations against male complacency. It is the curious fact that, at its appearance, this essay should have stirred critics to rare extremes of passion and partisanship. Loath to grant her even partial accuracy in her presentation, most critics at that time harped on minor details.

Viewed from the vantage point of our day, when much more radical books have been written in the meantime on these same problems, *The Second Sex* stands as a monument, the earliest consistent manifesto establishing women's role. Far from exonerating women in her survey, Beauvoir put the blame where it belonged with regard to women who behaved foolishly. But the upshot of her work is clearly the strong advocacy of systematizing women's rights.

The treatise, sometimes unwieldy, is nevertheless meaningful at every level. The essayist has reached into many social sciences and other disciplines in order to understand, for herself and for others, the complex interplay between the sexes over the whole gamut of prehistorical and historical development. In so doing, examples are used that are supportive of her point of view, naturally, but she never recoils from showing some women in a light other than favorable whenever it is a matter of integrity. On the whole, her illustrations are meant to corroborate her thesis—man is unjust to woman. Inevitably, there are cases where man is shown to be relatively guiltless in developments due to physiological conditions or where women lacked either the strength or the initiative to change their lot.

In listing, without outward passion, the many handicaps encountered by women, even in the matter of striking up friendships, the essayist indicates the male counterpart where no such difficulties exist. Her reasoning is solid. The elements of distinction between conditions for men and for women are firmly outlined. No verbal excesses are ever committed. That is why the ledger is even more heavily weighted against male complacency and injustice: even if individual men are not deliberately slighting women's role, inevitably they avoid giving thought to the many urgent problems that burden women down as wives, mothers, partners in marriage and in life.

Explaining the way women function, biologically, socially, psychologically, often as plain human beings caught up in a situation without alternatives, Beauvoir displays robust good sense. Women's whims appear much less capricious or eccentric when traced to needs; man's objections to women's inability to "do" things is fully shown to be of nature's making or of man's own making—witness Ibsen's Nora. Thus, for instance, plain talk about the ridiculous way

women dress—they do so only to please men—proves women could
be far better off with common sense shoes or some other article of
apparel.

Part Two of the first volume of the essay is devoted to history. In a
vast fresco, Beauvoir depicts male domination throughout. Wom-
en's misfortune, she states, is to have been stamped biologically in
order to create and "repeat life while in her own eyes life itself does
not contain a *raison d'être;* those reasons are more important than
life itself." An existential perspective, she continues, has enabled us
to understand how the biological and economic situation of primitive
hordes had to lead to male supremacy. Females are more than males
the prey of the species. "And," "she she asks, "what place has mankind
conceded to that part of itself which in its midst defined itself as the
other?" At the prehistoric stage, the author shows that life was not
the supreme value for man. Life had to serve ends more important
than itself: "The worst curse that was laid upon woman was that she
should be excluded from these warlike forays. For it is not in giving
life but in risking life that man is raised above the animal; that is
why superiority has been accorded in humanity not to the sex that
brings forth but to that which kills" (64).

From prehistory through antiquity, the essayist leads us to the
times when women missed the chance to be emancipated. In the
course of her exposition, she demolishes quite a few old myths; thus,
she attacks the cliché of matriarchate and shows by the example of
primitive matrimonial usages how woman was honored and charged
with essential social functions. On every continent, in every age,
she marks the progress of woman's formation. In Rome, for instance, on balance, woman's position was respected. At the same
time, the author shows the paradoxical inconsistencies of men's acts
throughout history:

At the very moment when woman, for all practical purposes is emancipated,
the inferiority of her sex is proclaimed, which is a remarkable example of
the male self-justification that I mentioned before. From the moment that
her rights as a daughter, spouse, sister are no longer limited, she is denied
equality with men as a member of her sex; in order to subject her, any
pretext of imbecility and frailty of her sex is good enough. (151)

VIII *Woman's Fate and Her Image*

The essayist pursues her analysis of woman's fate through the
barbarian invasions and during the spread of Christianity. She finds

that the Christian ideology contributed "not a little" to woman's oppression, in part probably because ever since Saint Paul's preachings, the fiercely antifeminist Jewish tradition was integrated into Christianity. The church fathers, too, perpetuated this hostility with respect to all women. The stagnation lasted throughout the Middle Ages. Only at the dawn of the Renaissance was there a first significant change for the better. Humanism brought with it reflections on women's place in society.

The Ancien Régime receives a measure of praise for its attitude toward women, whereas the revolution, despite the immense hopes for emancipation of women it furthered, did not bring justice in its path. Napoléon's reforms proved meager comfort, with decrees such as the one on divorce, canceled by the ensuing restoration.

The present summary of Simone de Beauvoir's elaboration does not do justice to her reasoning, which is far more subtle than this condensation could show it to be. Her historical presentation is competent and comprehensive. Thus, when she deals with the situation in the early days of the Industrial Revolution, she shows that employers preferred women to men for the simple reason that they did better work for a lesser salary. That cynical formula, she states, illustrates the drama of feminine labor. Women achieved their dignity as human beings through work, she recalls, but that achievement was singularly hard and slow to come by. And yet, in theory, women ought to have made better progress on account of that same evolution: "the coming of the machine destroyed landed property and furthered the emancipation of the working class along with that of women. All forms of socialism, wresting woman away from the family, favor her liberation" (112).

The third part of the essay is entitled "Myths." Among other major trends, Beauvoir points to the enormous contradictions in the image of woman as it was conceived at different times. Myths are difficult to describe, claims the author. They can never be pinpointed. There are ambivalences and contradictions all over the myth of woman: she is at one and the same time Dalila and Judith, Aspasia and Lucrecia, Pandora and Athena; woman is both Eva and the Virgin Mary; she is an idol, a servant; she is the source of life and the power of darkness. She is the elementary silence of truth and yet she also is artifice, chatter, and lies. She is, in turns, a healer and a witch.

Some of the poignant questions which these contradictions provoke have been receiving tentative answers before Beauvoir appeared on the scene. What she attempted to do is offer existentialist
explanations for a situation that poses existential problems:

> Woman has often been compared to water because, among other reasons,
> she is the mirror in which the male, Narcissus-like, contemplates himself:
> he bends over her in good or bad faith. But in any case what he really asks of
> her is to be outside of him, all that which he cannot grasp inside himself,
> because the inwardness of the existent is only nothingness and because he
> must project himself into an object in order to reach himself. Woman is the
> supreme recompense for him since, under a shape foreign to him which he
> can possess in her flesh, she is his own apotheosis. He embraces this "in-
> comparable monster" himself, when he presses in his arms the being who
> sums up the world for him and upon whom he has imposed his values and
> his laws. Then, in uniting with this other whom he has made his own, he
> hopes to reach himself. (185–86)

This rather dense piece of reasoning is followed by more examples
of woman's ambivalent image: "Treasure, prey, sport and danger,
nurse, guide, judge, mediatrix, mirror, woman is the Other in
whom the subject transcends himself without being limited, who
opposes him without denying him; she is the Other who lets herself
be taken without ceasing to be the Other . . ." (186).

More variations on the contradictory theme of the image of
woman appear after this one. The upshot is that there is no one and
only clear image. This is why the author is determined to help in
creating a working formula for an acceptable image that might satisfy
most standards. In so doing, she often overstates her case, in this
section of the book even more so than in the previous ones.

The fourth part of the book bears the title "The Formative Years,"
and Beauvoir proceeds to give a clear view, from the vantage point
of our day, of the factors that make women. The author displays
unusual caution in the writing of this section. What she proclaims
finding are not eternal truths but merely some elements of the
present stage of education and of moral conditions in our time.

"Women are not born but made," is but one of the discoveries
offered in this part of the essay. Among other considerations,
Beauvoir examines the different ways of experiencing separation
and weaning of childhood affection, as it is felt by boys and by girls.

Most of the psychoanalytical attempts at explaining "castration" and other complexes are reviewed sensibly. No doubt, Beauvoir went to such lengths in the psychoanalytical discussion of the comparative status respectively of male and female physical endowment mainly to exhaust all possibilities for a fair assessment given to male domination in sexual matters. She is fair, indeed, but the objective ledger must appear heavily tilted against women. For instance, the little girl already accepts as a given fact the physical prowess of her brother.

The conditioning of the girl for becoming a woman seems consistent, in the essayist's presentation. Through the wearing of clothing meant to underscore femininity; through tasks and chores in the home specifically reserved for girls rather than boys—in plain words, Beauvoir shows such conditioning to be one of the main factors for feminine subjection to male domination in our society, where equality, theoretically, is guaranteed. Man's prestige within the family is illustrated, even though it is the mother who reigns in actuality in the home; that is so, often, because she will be intelligent enough to decide everything in the father's name.

For an individual who feels as the subject in living, who feels autonomous, transcendent as an absolute, it is a strange experience, according to the author, to discover within one's self a given essential inferiority. For those who feel in their selves as One, it is a strange experience to be revealed in its otherness. That is what happens when in learning about her position in the world, the individual grasps the fact that she is to be a woman.

Simone de Beauvoir exposes the maze of contradictory, evasive, vague, grossly insufficient answers to any urgent questions on sex. Although essays like hers have contributed to some progress in the public interest in that problem and in the attempts at solving it, the situation still is far from enlightened even now, some thirty years later. School boards in the United States take differing views on sex education, and in France, the picture is not much brighter. Simone de Beauvoir concedes that even a coherent education could not in and by itself solve the problem overnight. With all the good intentions of parents and teachers, she writes, the erotic experience cannot be translated into words and concepts. It has to be lived. Any analysis, no matter how serious, would appear to have a humorous aspect and would fail to unveil the truth. In a like mood, tactfully and concisely, the author describes the reaction in either young men or young women to the sexual drive. Not a word in excess is used here; every idea is soberly stated and circumscribed.

IX Detachment and Sympathy; Involvement

The fourth part of the essay, "The Formative Years," had begun by analyzing the young girl. While the general remarks about childhood, including both normal and abnormal tendencies, were written from an all-encompassing, generally human point of view, this chapter starts out strictly from a middle class viewpoint. The essayist summarizes bourgeois prejudice, first seriously, then somewhat facetiously. One might say that Beauvoir is operating here with an involved sort of detachment.

The author proceeds to depict some of the apparent inconsistencies in young girls' attitudes, showing them as eager and proud of catching attention and causing admiration, yet, through a growing sense of shame, at the same time leery of male treachery: "Men's stares flatter and hurt her simultaneously; she wants only what shows to be seen: eyes are always too penetrating. She enjoys inflaming the male, but if she sees that she has aroused his desire, she recoils in disgust. Masculine desire is as much an offense as it is a compliment. . . ." (351).

The essayist chose strikingly plausible illustrations for her thesis. In describing the rapid change in feelings in the very young girl, she pulled no punches and showed the delicate fabric of adolescent sensitivities, but at the same time, the playfulness and coquetry that often lead to painful misunderstandings between members of opposite sexes. Her choice of Colette's novels for a portrait of this stage in adolescence is most felicitous, as Colette's heroines display just such uncertainties and anxieties, combined with the natural curiosity of their age.

In examining these contradictory trends, Beauvoir shows her detachment from partisan arguments. Her intense observation of both human nature and the scientific analysis of numerous cases, as she faithfully and at times pedantically recounts it, yields a rich harvest of revealing traits of this decisive stage in feminine evolution. The consequences of such analysis are to be felt in the author's treatment of mature women, where the same kind of scientific detachment can be observed. She is both the spokesman—if we may still call her that, what with linguistic sensitivities to old ways of speaking—and the umpire in the continuing battle between the sexes where objectivity is scarce.

The third chapter of part four is "Sexual Initiation," where, again, the author is interested only in the psychological framework of woman at a decisive moment of her life. Interestingly enough, Beauvoir displays a most competent use of linguistic skills in determining male prejudice and arrogance: military similes are used by men in describing their sexual encounters; images of contest, of wrestling, are frequently used, too. The harsh reality is refreshingly contrasted with the delicate complexity of feminine feelings in those circumstances. Feminine sexuality, in Simone de Beauvoir's analysis of it, is far more complicated than any normal man could suspect. It is therefore imperative that more men should read this essay. Even with growing awareness of the different reactions in either sex, many potential areas of misunderstanding will remain. The undeniable merit of *The Second Sex* is, among others, to serve as an eyeopener, even in this day and age, to both men and women.

Chapter four deals with the lesbian woman. Contrary to general assumptions, the lesbian phenomenon is decidedly not of physiological origin. The essayist sees no hard and fast lines between "normal" women and lesbians. Disappointment over male sexuality, difficulties in finding a man, availability of affection, and protection—these are some of the many diverse elements that can create the climate for the development leading to lesbianism. Lesbian leanings do not necessarily prevent "normal" relationships either, says the author. The conclusion is stated in crisp, cool terms, characteristic of Beauvoir's approach to dealing with matters long considered taboo: "The truth is that homosexuality is no more a perversion deliberately indulged in than it is a curse of fate. It is an *attitude chosen in a certain situation*—that is, at once motivated and freely adopted" (424).

X *Changes*

The first chapter of the second volume is entitled "The Married Woman." The author posits certain changes within the "institution" of marriage, some for economic reasons, some for other, mostly social or psychological ones. In spite of the apparent equality that marriage contracts stipulate, there is "no symmetry in the situation" of husband and wife. Searching for the underlying causes of this dissymmetry, Beauvoir writes:

Since the husband is the productive worker, he is the one who goes beyond family interest to that of society, opening up a future for himself through co-operation in the building of the collective future: he incarnates transcendence. Woman is doomed to the continuation of the species and the care of the home—that is to say, to immanence. (429)

Analyzing some of the elements of that immanence, the essayist points to household cleaning work as an end in itself which is often offering an evasion from reality. With even greater insight, the author traces the role of wife, from timid beginnings to all-controlling jealousy where she dictates to her husband what to do. She indicates the impossible position in the provinces as well as in Paris, of the housewife, pressed—or compressed—between chores and social obligations, sexually uncertain, yet domineering and at times threatened by others.

The whole chapter on the married woman is excellent. It proves that anybody finding fault with Beauvoir's psychology and method would have to go far afield to pinpoint any shortcomings. Not being a spouse or a mother never prevents the essayist from using good judgment and excellent documentation.

The second chapter, "The Mother," deals among other matters with abortion, a grave and massive problem. Eloquent statistics show how inane and hostile to the poor existing legislation is. Some individual examples make a persuasive case against this backward aspect of the law. Besides, the psychological impact is immeasurable wherever women are confronted with an impossible choice:

Men tend to take abortion lightly; they regard it as one of the numerous hazards imposed on women by malignant nature, but fail to realize fully the values involved. The woman who has recourse to abortion is disowning feminine values, her values, and at the same time is in most radical fashion running counter to the ethics established by men. Her whole moral universe is disrupted. . . . Even when she consents to abortion, even desires it, woman feels it as a sacrifice of her femininity: she is compelled to see in her sex a curse, a kind of infirmity, and a danger. . . . (491)

Speaking of the woman as mother of the child, the writer gives an interesting and original analysis for the role of the husband's mother. A sense of guilt is often found to be inspired by the mother-in-law, whose influence may become nefarious in certain situations: still-born infants and other accidents bring about occasional hatred against the mother-in-law. Pregnancies and births are of course experienced in widely differing ways according to the psychological disposition of the mother.

While this demonstration seems flawless, certain statements of the author's are clearly excessive: "no maternal 'instinct' exists: the word hardly applies in any case to the human species" (511). The education of the child brings with it new problems confronting the mother. A latent ambivalence makes the mother hesitant, in many cases, as to the education of a son, while no such hesitation exists for the daughter. Simone de Beauvoir's reasoning deserves to be heard on this situation: showing that the mother's influence on her son may tend to be negative, the author lists some of the ambivalent attitudes:

> It is too rational, too simple, to believe that she would like to castrate her son; her dream is more contradictory: she would have him of unlimited power, yet held in the palm of her hand, dominating the world, yet on his knees before her. She encourages him to be soft, greedy, generous, timid, quiet, she forbids sport and playmates, she makes him lack self-confidence, because she intends to *have* him for herself; but she is disappointed if at the same time he fails to become an adventurer, a champion, a genius worthy of her pride. There is no doubt her influence is often injurious . . . Fortunately for the boy, he can rather easily escape the toils . . . And the mother herself is resigned to it, for she knows very well that the struggle against man is an unequal one. . . . she is proud she is to have engendered one of her conquerors. (517)

Thus Beauvoir weights the balance against women, who are shown to be sometimes less than rational. On the other hand, the author points to woman's competence in the counsels of family or even of government. Whereas man is said to be at his best outside the home, and less capable of emotional control at home, the woman

> if she is given opportunity, . . . is as rational, as efficient, as a man; it is in abstract thought, in planned action, that she rises most easily above her sex. It is much more difficult, *as things are*, for her to escape from her woman's past, to attain an emotional balance that nothing in her situation favors. . . . It would clearly be desirable for the good of the child if the mother were a complete, unmutilated person, a woman finding in her work and in her relation to society a self-realization that she would not seek to attain tyrannically through her offspring. . . . (524)

This thought process climaxes in the rather legitimate speculation: "In a properly organized society, where children would be
largely taken in charge by the community and the mother cared for
and helped, maternity would not be wholly incompatible with
careers for women" (525). Such a development is indeed sought
after even today in the United States, where the demand for day
care centers is heard everywhere.

Chapter Three, "Social Life," deals with the many practical
problems confronting women, such as dress, social invitations, hos-
pitality. With a fine ear for linguistic distinctions, Beauvoir notes
that woman "must make a good showing" and "dress up." For men,
clothes need not attract attention, she writes. "Woman, on the contrary, is even required by society to make herself an erotic object"
(529). In this vein, the author analyzes fashions that force women to
wear clothes that are by and large inconvenient in order to stress
feminine assets. "Confronting man," she writes, "woman is always
play-acting; she lies when she makes believe that she accepts her
status as the inessential other" (543).

The conflict between the sexes is emphasized by the essayist to
the highest point. Thus, she considers women as being for one another like fellow prisoners, helping one another to bear their captivity
and even to prepare their escape. The liberator, however, will
come from the male world—a rather surprising, defeatist remark.

In much the same vein, concluding the chapter on social life, the
author thinks that adultery, friendships, society life are, within the
framework of conjugal life, but pastimes; they may help to bear its
constraints but never break them. These are all false escapes which
do not at all allow women to reshape their own destiny, the writer
contends.

The next chapter, four, deals with prostitutes. Beauvoir sees an
affinity between the great "cocottes" and great stars of stage and
screen. Both spend most of their time in sheer boredom, "dense
ennui." Chapter five goes from "Maturity to Old Age." One of the
elements noted here is the frenetic desire to live, to change, "the
last opportunity." From this delicate situation comes the disposition, quite frequent at the stage of menopause, to become devout
and even to join all sorts of sects. Mothers grow even more demanding on their sons and go through all sorts of ambivalences,
ambitions, and fears. These ambivalences include their relation to

their grandchildren; to be a grandmother is to be closer to death, in some ways, as Hegel has said. Women join clubs and share in ladies' charities and activities.

Chapter six speaks of "Woman's Situation and Character." Reviewing the history of women, Beauvoir sees that their condition has remained the same through superficial changes. All the usual clichés coined by men against women are listed: "she 'revels in immanence,' she is contrary, she is prudent and petty, she has no sense of fact or accuracy, she lacks morality, she is contemptibly utilitarian, she is false, theatrical, self-seeking. . ." (597). The author concedes that there is an element of truth in all this. But, she insists, "the varieties of behavior reported are not dictated to woman by her hormones nor predetermined in the structure of the female brain: they are shaped as in a mold by her situation" (597).

Faithful to existentialist reasoning, Beauvoir is tackling woman's economic, social, and historical conditioning. Using the full range of her not inconsiderable psychological knowledge, she quite lyrically at times traces the way women may conquer their problems. The only liberation the essayist envisions is a collective one, solving with one fell swoop every woman's difficulties.

In this section, through circuitous perspectives, the writer manages to see the question in turn from woman's and from man's point of view. However, the very fairness with which she operates this overview makes an even stronger indictment of injustices than woman's complaint alone would have wrought.

The second part of this second volume bears the title "Justifications," and its first chapter is "The Narcissistic Woman." Two converging roads, the author claims, lead to narcissism. As a subject, woman feels frustrated. Her "aggressive sexuality" remains unsatisfied. Male activities are inaccessible to her. She keeps busy, but actually does nothing. Even in her functions as spouse, mother, housekeeper, she is not recognized in her singularity. So she is doomed to immanence and repetition.

Chapter two is on "Woman in Love." Simone de Beauvoir runs through the whole gamut of attachment and jealousy. She comments on woman's insistence on asking man, at the most unpropitious moment, whether he loves her, without giving him time to react in a subtly graded reply. The essayist brushes a masterful tableau, fair and full, describing the suffering through jealousy and a possessiveness that is inevitable yet counterproductive. Her psychological insight proves sure-footed. Her dealing with these delicate matters is firm and sensitive at the same time.

Chapter three deals with "The Mystique." Love has been assigned, the author says, to woman as an all-encompassing vocation. Some men are also prone to burn with the same fire, but they are rather rare and their passion assumes an intellectual, purified form. Woman, Beauvoir writes, is used to living on her knees. Mystical fervor, just like love and even narcissism, the writer claims, may become integrated into active and independent lives. But by and in themselves, those efforts to secure individual salvation could only end in failure. Woman either seeks rapport with something unreal, her own double or God, or she creates an unreal rapport with a real being; in either case, she has no grasp on the world, she never escapes her subjectivity. Her freedom remains "mystified." There is only one way to achieve freedom authentically, and that is by positive action, projecting into human society.

The third part of volume two, "Toward Liberation," has as its first and only chapter "The Independent Woman," which spells out what had become clear over the course of Beauvoir's demonstration in this work: "It is through gainful employment that woman has traversed most of the distance that separated her from the male; and nothing else can guarantee her liberty in practice. Once she ceases to be a parasite, the system based on her dependence crumbles . . ." (679).

Sharply militant, for once, Beauvoir displays a keen critical sense in her exposition of feminism. She shows that women engaged in the battle for independence have to pay a double penalty in their greater efforts to equal men. The woman who wants her freedom and is ready to fight for it wants to live both as a man and as a woman; this multplies her tasks and chores and increases her fatigue. But other obstacles arise on the steep path to independence. In France, Beauvoir reminds us, there is a stubborn attitude in men, who like to mistake the free woman for the facile one.

The author's detached way of writing on matters close to her heart is best evidenced in the pages where she assesses the role of woman writers:

a literature of protest can engender sincere and powerful works; out of the well of her revolt, George Eliot drew a vision of Victorian England that was at once detailed and dramatic; still, as Virginia Woolf has made us see, Jane Austen, the Brontë sisters, George Eliot, have had to expend so much energy negatively in order to free themselves from outward restraints that they arrive somewhat out of breath at the stage from which masculine writers of great scope take their departure; they do not have enough strength left to profit by their victory and break all the ropes that hold them back. We do not find in them, for example, the irony, the ease of a Stendhal, nor his calm sincerity. Nor have they had the richness of experience of a Dostoyevsky, a Tolstoy: this explains why the splendid *Middlemarch* still is not the equal of *War and Peace*; *Wuthering Heights*, in spite of its grandeur, does not have the sweep of *The Brothers Karamazov*. (709)

It took courage and forthrightness to recognize what, in the historical development, lacked in women through no fault of theirs. It makes the case the essayist built so patiently and eloquently for women's rights even more convincing. As she put it very simply: "Today it is already less difficult for women to assert themselves but they have not as yet completely overcome the agelong sex-limitation that has isolated them in their femininity" (709).

Reverting for a moment to the comparative study of man's and woman's possibilities, Beauvoir contemplates what makes man the creator in so many fields. For all their flaws, men were able to project their thoughts toward action and thus build ahead, assuming an enormous burden in the making of our world. Women were not able, the essayist states, to claim their share in the position of the privileged. And she asks a question that is amazing to hear coming from a woman writer's pen:

How could Van Gogh have been born a woman? A woman would not have been sent on a mission to the Belgian coal mines. . . . she would not have felt the misery of the miners as her own crime, she would not have sought a redemption; she would therefore have never painted Van Gogh's sunflowers. Not to mention that the mode of life of the painter—his solitude at Arles, his frequentation of cafés and brothels, all that nourished Van Gogh's art in nourishing his sensitivity—would have been forbidden her. A woman would never have become Kafka. . . . (713)

With biting irony, Beauvoir writes a conclusion that caps the work most fittingly. To those who throw up their arms, hypocritically pitying woman's deprivation in her factual enslavement to man, she retorts that the theory of "low-class gain" has had its day: "In France, also, it has often been proclaimed—although in a less scientific manner—that workers are very fortunate in not being obliged to 'keep up appearances' and still more so the bums who can dress in rags and sleep on the sidewalks, pleasures forbidden to the Count de Beaumont and the Wendels" (720).

Rather than a summary, Beauvoir offers a hopeful perspective, ending in the demand that men and women unequivocally assert their solidarity.

XI   An Icebreaker at Work

Clearing the air by speaking for woman, Beauvoir has done a great and good service to mankind. In maintaining a fair and balanced view of woman's potential over against her set status, the author has proven that a woman thinker has the same powers of mind as men who often neglected to take women's demands seriously. Not nearly all the blame is put on men, and here, too, Beauvoir evidences great skill and superb judgment, making her findings available to all, men and women alike. As time goes by, fewer and fewer male critics can find fault with her argument, since it is couched in terms of reasonableness and moderation.

It is likely that no one scientific discipline may agree wholly on the methods used and the results achieved by Beauvoir in this book. After all, the essayist had been concerned mainly with describing conditions as she saw them after a thorough and sincere investigation. The product of her search is a strong indictment of prejudice, but free from partisan zeal and almost entirely without aggressive overtones.

What contradictions she noted in the feminine mind do, of course, exist just as copiously in man's mind. Perhaps the writer was too discreet, the former teacher too patient to spell this out. It is, however, imperative to note this fact, implicit in the pages of the essay, and Beauvoir, as a true disciple of Montaigne and Pascal, could not impugn it. It is the human heart and mind that are subject to contradiction, regardless of sex.

On the concrete side, The Second Sex stands as a solid achievement in its earnest treatment of one of the major problems of all times. Throughout the book, Beauvoir knew how to illustrate rather than to plead, to show and convince rather than to scold. Hers is the finest contribution to the effective freeing of woman. Now the road to even more progress is open, thanks to her pioneering effort, her measured advocacy of reason and good sense. The Second Sex remains one of her best works, the least likely to become obsolete, despite the rapid pace of scientific discovery and the immense amount of publications on the question of women. Her data may go out of fashion. Her ideas stand and are as clear and cogent as at the time of her writing.

XII   La Vieillesse (The Coming of Age, *1970*)

About twenty-five years separate the publication of this book from that of *The Second Sex*. Never one to tire of examining the condition of the underprivileged, Beauvoir had touched upon basic questions concerning the aged in her earlier great essay. Again, in the new treatise, she views the fundamental problem to be one of society as a whole, inseparable from the lot of the workers or from social justice altogether. That is why the treatment given the question of old age is very much like that accorded women in its earnest pursuit of truth, in the determination to work for progress and equity in an area too long neglected.

Though her findings point an accusing finger at existing conditions, both in Western countries and, to some extent, even in socialist states, the more recent work shows equanimity to a greater extent than most previous essays by Beauvoir. The situation depicted is grim; the attitude of most nations toward their aged, in the modern world, is still flawed with inconsistencies. Yet the author is careful to record every bit of progress achieved over the years and avoids wholesale condemnation of those in a position of power and responsibility, while denouncing the slowness of change and the inadequacy of care for old people.

Her concern is really with the old people, so long the victims of neglect and lack of understanding. She is eager to convey as full and telling a picture of the aged as could be assembled through the study of history and anthropology and through the analysis of the various ways in which mankind has tried to cope with old people or failed to even give thought to their existence. The result is a full-fledged dossier containing both general documentation on the historical aspect of the question and a finely individualized examination of the most representative cases, showing old people to be a most diversified group with an enormous spread of diverging tendencies. The dossier is used to demand reforms in the ways old people are dealt with. Since in the essayist's eyes, the matter of old age cannot be divorced from the total picture of social justice, her stand recalls her basic militancy in *The Second Sex*, where, too, the blame never was laid on any single group but on an accumulation of bad practices and attitudes. Just as the male world, in the earlier essay, was not alone in sustaining the blame, so no particular generation of adults is being accused of having neglected to come to terms with the solution to old age. Even though Beauvoir may contradict herself in some small instances, her aim is clear, her tendency sound, her argumentation straightforward and persuasive. *The Coming of Age* is in many ways a more balanced book than *The Second Sex*. It may never cause as much controversy as the essay on women, but it does not lack vigor and clarity. If male readers of *The Second Sex* came away with a feeling of guilt, any human being should get an uncomfortable sense of shame, of failure, when confronted with the tragic situation of the old people in Beauvoir's description. In this connection, is is significant that, nine years after the publication of *The Coming of Age*, the French government still refuses to show a serious documentation on old age on the state-run television system: Simone de Beauvoir, and Marianne Ahrne and Pépo Angel, have made a film, *Promenade au Pays de la Vieillesse (A Walk through the Country of Old People)* in which they show, rather graphically, the dereliction afflicting old people in hospitals and retirement homes.[14]

XIII *From the Particular to the General*

One of Beauvoir's recent critics, Robert Cottrell, notes that in *The Second Sex*, while analyzing the situation of women in general, the author was preparing the way for a study of a particular woman—herself. "Seen in this light," Cottrell writes, *"Le Deuxième Sexe* is a long preamble to the four volumes of the autobiography she would write later." Interestingly, he adds, the last of the four volumes, *Tout Compte Fait*, a book in which the author meditates on her old age, "was preceded by another weighty sociological study, *La Vieillesse*. Here too the general study is followed by an examination of her own particular case."[15]

There is much validity in this assessment. The essayist has never made any bones about her involvement in situations of social concern, or about her illustrations being increasingly chosen from her own life—for example, her experience with Zaza's death. Just how far the general is only a shield, or a first step, for the particular is a matter of appreciation. It seems to me that her interest in people in general is genuine and far too lively to be only a pretext for a personal project. In fact, Cottrell does not suggest that either, and it would seem that, indeed, the practice of essay writing before fictionalizing or writing autobiographical material is not limited to Beauvoir. Camus, for one, found it fruitful to sort his ideas in a searching essay before tackling these same ideas, in different ways, in novels, witness *The Myth of Sisyphus*, preceding *The Stranger*.

The change of focus is a most felicitous technique, enabling the author to inject a note of immediacy into writings that might otherwise assume an air of aloofness. The study of old age obviously had haunted the author over the years, as she became aware of the ageing process in herself and others and as she continued to meditate on death. For, as Elaine Marks has shown in her probing study, very early in life, Beauvoir had been affected by the awareness of death and had integrated into novels, essays, and memoirs alike her constant preoccupation with it.

The author readily lets us know her reasons for writing this book. In the introduction, she states that she means to break the "conspiracy of silence" that society is perpetuating about old age. In France, twelve per cent of the population are over sixty-five, and where the proportion of old people is the highest in the world, "they are condemned to poverty, decrepitude, wretchedness and despair. In the United States, their lot is no happier."[16] So the writer sets out to do something about the unwillingness of society to cope with this huge problem: "I shall compel my readers to hear the voices of those who are, . . . after all, human" (9).

The time at which old age begins is ill-defined. It varies, according to era and place. Where old age is concerned, no clear-cut transition from one age to the next exists. At the time the book was published, the aged did not yet form a group having any political or economic strength. Since then, large associations have been formed in the United States for precisely the purpose of enforcing the rights of old people.

Old age has been acclaimed, the writer says, as offering a model of all the virtues—hence, the old are required to live up to those standards. Popular usage associates old age with degradation and decay. The essayist notes that, whether they be admired for their venerable air, their white hair, or mocked for being no longer fully functioning, old people "stand outside humanity." The world, therefore, need feel no scruple in refusing them "the minimum of

support which is considered necessary for living like a human being"
(11).

Mortality is acknowledged by people more readily, in general,
than ageing. "Nothing," Beauvoir writes, "should be more expected than old age: nothing is more unforeseen" (12). She reminds
us that to think of oneself as an old person when one is twenty or
forty means thinking of oneself as someone else, as another than
oneself. "Until the moment it is upon us," she states, "old age is
something that only affects other people" (13). She goes on, warning
us: "We must stop cheating: the whole meaning of our life is in
question in the future that is waiting for us. If we do not know what
we are going to be, we cannot know what we are: let us recognize
ourselves in this old man or that old woman" (13–14).

Much in the vein of her analysis of woman in *The Second Sex*,
where society as a whole was taken to task for its failure to cope with
woman's status, she sees the problem of the aged in the framework
of the whole of society. "The fact that for the last fifteen or twenty
years of his life, a man should be no more than a reject, a piece of
scrap reveals the failure of our civilization" (15; cf. pp. 804–805). But
mere condemnation of the "maiming, crippling system in which we
live" is not enough. She demands that we expose "this scandal" (15).
And again, in concluding her introduction, . Beauvoir states co-
gently and forcefully that the problem of ageing needs to be seen in
the context of justice for society as a whole. That is, she claims, why
the "whole problem is so carefully passed over in silence" (16). To
shatter this silence, she calls upon her readers for their help.

In the preface, viewing the complexities in any attempt at definition of old age, the author declares that her study must try to be
exhaustive. That is why, her essential aim being to show the fate of
the old in our present-day society, she devotes "so many pages to
the place they occupy in what are called primitive communities . . .
In order to judge our own society we have to compare the solutions
it has chosen with those adopted by others through space and time.
This comparison will allow us to distinguish that which is inescapable in the state of the aged; to see how far and at what cost these
hardships can be eased; and hence to gauge the responsibility of the
system in which we live with respect to these hardships" (18–19).

She considers both the outsider's view of old people and the
subjective concept of old people about themselves. The first viewpoint is to guide her in the first part of the book, where biology,

anthropology, history, and contemporary sociology will help in examining old age. In the second part, the aged man "inwardly apprehends his relationship with his body, with time, and with the outside world" (19). She is frank enough to concede that neither of these two inquiries will enable one to define old age per se.

In the introduction and in the preface, Beauvoir made an attempt at elaborating ground rules for the analysis and discussion of old age, only to discover that the shifting sands of perpetually changing conditions may keep her forever from achieving any ruling that might be considered general and universally valid. Her essay, quite similar in this respect to *The Second Sex*, will make it impossible to go back to the status quo: nobody can pretend to ignore old age after Simone de Beauvoir has opened our eyes and our minds to the fearful reality.

XIV *Is Our Society Better Than "Primitive" Community?*

Part One begins with a chapter on "Old Age Seen From Without." In this biological survey, we learn that there was slow and halting progress in medicine, generally, and in geriatrics in particular, up to the early nineteenth century. With the sudden growth in numbers among the aged, all sorts of theories on the process of ageing were elaborated. Even as late as around the turn of the century, "a few scientists still hoped, as their predecessors in earlier times had done, to explain the process of ageing by a single cause" (35). With the repeated doubling of the numbers of aged persons in the United States in the twentieth century, rapid progress was being made in gerontology here.

Chapter two, "The Ethnological Data," examines the place of the old in a number of species, in particular among anthropoid apes, where the ageing male chieftain is eclipsed by younger ones. In early human societies—as indeed at all times—age makes man unproductive, and he represents a burden. But, the essayist points out, in certain societies where the grown man determines the lot of the old, he at the same time chooses his own future: "he therefore takes his own long-term interest into consideration" (65).

That, of course, is already a development based on complex thought processes. The status of the old was established empirically. In most primitive societies the aged became a burden; they were neglected or ill-treated. Their death, be it voluntary or not, seems usual. In only a few tribes there are links of affection, of respect. In certain countries, the old practice magic and have religious attributes enabling them to continue living.

Some of Simone de Beauvoir's deductions sound like truisms; yet, in order to discover these, she had to study a large number of documents. She writes: "Happy children tend to grow into adults honoring their parents and ancestors" (89). She found only one exception to the rule—the Ojibway—where happy children turn into adults who are cruel to their fathers and mothers. Old age, the writer reminds us, sets men apart, so that they form a distinct category. In primitive societies, "the old man is necessary: he is also dangerous, because he may turn his magic knowledge to his own advantage. There is still another cause for this ambivalence—seeing that he is close to death he is also close to the supernatural world" (123). The chapter culminates in a conclusion that ties primitive society to our own, and the comparison is not flattering for our time:

The practical solutions adopted by primitive people to deal with the problems set by their old people are very varied: the old are killed; they are left to die; they are given a bare minimum to support life; a decent end is provided for them; or they are revered and cherished. As we shall see what are called civilized nations apply the same methods: killing alone is forbidden, unless it is disguised. (131)

Chapter three is "Old Age in Historical Societies." "The aged," declares the author, "considered as social categories, have never influenced the progress of the world" (132–33). She allows for particular cases of old men and old women who have played active roles. If one observes that during the First World War, for example, the men at the helm in France were old, some of them very old— she herself will study the case of Clemenceau—the particular seems to be overshadowed by the general in that these statesmen affected the course of the war and in a large measure the future of the world. Add to this that French as well as German soldiers who had to do the fighting and dying resented the superpatriotism of the old: Barrès, for one, was thunderstruck to see the indignation, the hatred that his name evoked in young people over his unqualified support of continued war. The old seemed dead set against the young in that period.

Beauvoir announced that her study will be limited, substantially, to the Western world, with the exception of China (where family structure created a pattern unlike that in any other country, favoring the reign of the old), "because of the uniquely privileged position that it provided for its old men" (135). Scrutinizing biblical laws and usages, Beauvoir sees that "the submission of the children must have been less absolute than it was in China: the Jewish society was far less rigorously organized, and it left more room for individualism" (140).

XV   *The Rejuvenation of the Gods*

Studying Greek antiquity, the author raises the question whether the fact that Greek literature and history "often echo the conflict between the young and the old, the sons and the fathers" (144), meant that the old men had a high position that was subsequently wrenched from them. The essayist notes that the ancient gods as they grew old become more and more unbearable ("méchants et pervertis") and that "this ends by causing a revolt that dethrones them. From that time on almost all the gods who rule over the world are young" (146).

Despite the inevitable rebellion of young against old, age retained much of its prestige. For Homer, the idea of honor was attached to old age; age represented wisdom. Sparta was ruled by the *gerontes:* "Semantics seem to show that in remote antiquity the notion of honour was attached to that of old age. *Gera, geron:* the words that mean great age also mean the privilege of age, the rights of seniority, representative position" (147). Athens had the Areopage, and Solon acknowledged the soundness of such institutions. Poets, on the other hand, had ambivalent feelings toward age.

Taking a general view of classical antiquity, the author holds that: "What matters is the power held by the older generation. The middle-aged men's attitude toward this generation is ambiguous; they look to it for support in order to maintain a state of affairs advantageous to their class, and in the person of the wealthy old man they respect the holy rights of property" (184). Class reasons, one has to agree with the essayist, are what determine attitudes with regard to old people. The social underpinnings of prejudice are just as solid here as they proved to be with regard to women. Scorn and neglect are heaped on the aged, except where an awareness dawns that these very oldsters are the mirror image of ourselves, tomorrow.

XVI *The Young Rule the World*

During and after the barbarian invasion, the church adapted to the usage of different peoples. It made one positive contribution to the welfare of old people, the author notes: from the fourth century onwards, it built asylums and hospitals. The old no doubt were helped by these creations. However, during the Lower Empire and the early Middle Ages, "old men were almost entirely shut out of public life: it was the young who ruled the world" (190). Even popes were chosen young, with very few exceptions. The literature of the Middle Ages was not interested in old men; Charlemagne is the lone important exception. "Among the nobles, physical strength was of the first importance, just as it was among the peasants: there was no room for the weak" (196). Only one state was the exception; in Venice, the doge was old.

Beauvoir emphasizes an important shift in the pictorial representation of the trinity: Christ's role is more and more marked. "This supremacy of the Son over the Father grows steadily stronger from the eleventh century onwards" (200). The notion of time follows a parallel evolution. "Time, in that it is the enemy of life, is allied to death" (210). With Christ at the center of attention and the Virgin Mary the object of increasing general devotion, childhood, adolescence and above all, maturity were sanctified. "Old age was forgotten" (213).

The writer pauses to view the stereotyped manner in which old age had been handled from ancient Egypt to the Renaissance. She finds the same comparisons, the same adjectives used through the ages to describe old people:

These clichés persisted partly because the old person does in fact follow his unchangeable biological destiny; but also because, not being an active element in history, the old person was of no interest—no one took the trouble to study him as he really was. . . . In relation to youth and maturity [old age] was looked upon as a kind of foil or set-off: the old person was not true man, man himself, but rather man's further boundary; he was on the periphery of the human state; he was not acknowledged and no observer acknowledged himself in him. (243).

Shakespeare, too, proved ambivalent on the question of old age. He followed the trend of his time in his sonnets and in many situations in his plays. *King Lear* is the only great work, except for *Oedipus at Colonus*, Beauvoir states, in which the hero is an old man. Here, old age is not thought of as the limit of the human state but as its truth—"it is the basis for an understanding of man and his earthly pilgrimage" (245).

After the Council of Trent, the popes, too, were usually chosen old. The seventeenth century was very hard on children and on old people. Simone de Beauvoir gives us an intelligently condensed view of the exacting conditions during that century:

The average length of life was from twenty to twenty-five years. Half the children died before they were a year old, and most adults between thirty and forty. Exhausting labour, undernourishment and bad hygiene meant that people wore out very early. A peasant woman of thirty was a bent, wrinkled old woman. Even kings, nobles and burgesses died at between forty-eight and fifty-six. Public life began at seventeen or eighteen and promotion started early. Men in their forties were looked upon as old fogies. . . . There was no longer any place in society for a fifty-year-old . . . ." (249–50)

Her documentation rests on history, sociological and economic treatises, and a searching study of literature. Looking at Spanish views on the problem of old age, the author shows us Quevedo, who painted a misanthropic picture of old people; especially old women were the butt of his humor. In France, opinions were less biting but not much more favorable. Where Corneille had given some old men stature in his plays, for example Don Diègue in *Le Cid*, and the elder Horace, Molière did not deviate from the conventional treatment he inherited from the Commedia dell'Arte. His old men are mostly ridiculous, selfish, mean. Only occasionally, one of them would make up for the foolishness of the old types by his reasonable attitude, contrasting with the foibles of the others.

The eighteenth century saw some improvement in the form of the friendly societies, the first form of mutual aid and insurance. In France, the rehabilitation of the child began when Rousseau's writings became known. As Beauvoir put it: "The adults recognized themselves in the old people that they were to become" (272). Yet at about the same time, Swift had a completely different experience. His health ruined, grown misanthropic in his old age, he envisioned ageing as a lonely exile and the old person as a stranger, indeed a

foreigner in his own country. In France again, Voltaire was celebrated as the patriarch of Ferney. In the early stages of the French
Revolution, old people occupied the place of honor.

Demographic growth in the nineteenth century wrought important changes in society. The industrial revolution precipitated and
exacerbated social developments that were to create enormous
problems everywhere. In the United States, Beauvoir writes,
Taylorism meant havoc—all the workers died before their time.

XVII   *Experience No Longer Counts*

The restoration in France meant gerontocracy, and the revolution
of 1830 did nothing to change that order of things, since most rich
men were old. In the countryside, the patriarchal family continued
to exist, "and the authority of the old man who ruled it might be
tyrannical" (288). Generally speaking, in France and throughout the
Western world, the conflict between the generations vanished as far
as the bourgeoisie was concerned—a view of social history that
scarcely surprises readers of Simone de Beauvoir.

The twentieth century brought changes of a different nature: "A
striking fact . . . is that the standing of old age has been markedly
lowered since the notion of experience has been discredited. Modern technocratic society thinks that knowledge does not accumulate
with the years, but grows out of date. Age brings disqualification
with it: age is not an advantage. It is the values associated with youth
that are esteemed" (312–313).

In our time, Beauvoir states with obvious good reason, on account
of the "mass of documentary evidence that we have on the present
state of the aged" (313), literature no longer is as necessary and
valuable a source of information on this subject as it had been.
Psychological interest in literary illustrations of old age is as keen as
ever, and in the works of Ionesco and Beckett in particular, we find
a number of types of old people that are significant as messages to
the audience.

It had not been the aim of the author to give an outline of the
history of old age; all she intended to do was to describe the attitudes of historic societies toward old people "and the attitudes
they have worked out for themselves" (317). She remarks that old
people belonged to an unproductive minority and that their fate
depended upon the interests of the active majority. When it suited
the majority to establish intermediaries or representative figures

upon whose authority all could agree, the aged fulfilled these conditions, and there were times when they were called upon. The chapter concludes by emphasis on what had been declared all along: "Far more than the conflict between the generations, it was the class struggle that gave the notion of old age its ambivalence" (320).

Chapter four, "Old Age in Present-day Society," starts in exactly the same tonality: seeing that the condition of old people today is scandalous, Beauvoir wonders how adults could remain indifferent toward the lot of the aged, when "every single member of the community must know that his future is in question" (321), and almost all of them have close relatives among the old: "How can their attitude be explained? It is the ruling class that imposes their status upon the old, but the active population as a whole connives at it" (321).

The difficulties of ageing workers are compounded by prejudice against older people in employment situations. Yet, investigations and statistics in the matter of efficiency, reliability, regularity, prove that with increasing age reliability and regularity increase and that older people in general work conscientiously and well. Little is done, in most Western countries, to take these findings into account, and age prejudice continues unabated, legislation to combat these practices to the contrary. Ageing workers would not need to look for employment if their retirement brought them adequate resources. The conditions of pensioners are shameful in most countries studied by the essayist. In particular, the situation of widows is deplorable. Many retired people are living on a level near famine, and there are, in fact, a number of deaths attributable to starvation.

With regard to the United States, Beauvoir emphasizes the disadvantages of the capitalist system for the aged: by a generalized fear of "socialism," both state and federal government agencies hesitated a long time before the first timid steps were taken to remedy the pitiful conditions of old people. The author notes what Social Security does and does not do and weighs the advantages of Medicare and Medicaid and their inadequacies as they appeared in 1969.

In a more general way, she surveys the problem of housing for the old, studying the cases of those living alone and the ones living with their children or other relatives or friends. "The problem of housing is bound up with that of loneliness" (370), she writes after pointing to the dangers of old age depression and the frequency of suicides or simply of deaths due, one way or another, to depressing conditions.

Pursuing her investigation with extraordinary energy, Beauvoir visited several of the retirement homes and, particularly, hospitals and hospices where she found indescribable misery among the old.

Even with the best of intentions, she writes, hospitals are run in ways that are not to the old people's best interests. In the most modern, up to date institutions, she found conditions far from satisfactory; above all, it is the sense of isolation old people in institutions often have, and conversely, the complete lack of privacy: "not an inch of space he can call his own" (381). Residents of public old age homes are "never alone," to the point where that circumstance affects their minds. Even the cleanest, friendliest, prettiest hospice shows "total abjection" (386). The result, in the best cases, is listlessness in the old resident, who becomes a mere organism and suffers in a state of spiritual dereliction. The main contributing factor to this sad state of affairs is the absence of any occupation. Few of the trained staff have time to devote to any other than the most urgent duties, and many elderly people resent being abandoned to their own devices: they simply stay in bed or otherwise demonstrate their passive protest against being separated from society. Very few can be found who do anything at all with the unlimited time they have. No wonder that the writer deduces from such observations that "mere survival is worse than death" (407), as activities are indispensable for old people like any one else.

The tragedy of old age is tantamount to a fundamental condemnation of a whole mutilating system of life that provides the immense majority of those who make part of it with no reason for living. Labour and weariness hide this void: it becomes apparent as soon as they have retired. It is far more serious than boredom. Once the worker has grown old he no longer has any place on earth because in fact he was never given one. No place: but he had no time to realize it. When he does discover the truth he falls into a kind of bewildered despair. (410)

And as she had said in her introduction, the author restates that "old and poor is almost a tautology" (410). To some people, she adds, "their condition is so unbearable that they prefer death to the torment of living" (411). The number of suicides among the old is staggering.

XVIII *From Outside View to Inside Perspective*

Opening the second part of her book, the writer remarks that up to now she had viewed the aged from the outside, as an object.

Henceforth, she proposes to examine "what happens to the individual's relationship with his body and his image during his last years, to his relationship with time, history and his own praxis, and to his relationship with others and with the outside world" (415).

"The Being-in-the-World" is the title of the second part; chapter five is "The discovery and assumption of old age; the body's experience." It starts with the words: "Die early or grow old: there is no other alternative" (419). Yet, each and every one of us is astonished when we notice our growing old. "Old age is the general fate, and when it seizes upon our own personal life we are dumbfounded" (419). The author tries to sort out old people's subjective views about their health, and she comes up with a picture that is as diversified as any expression of opinions at any time. More people think of themselves as being in bad health after they are sixty, according to one report, but another survey gives a diametrically opposite view. Simone de Beauvoir tends to agree with Galen's idea that old age is halfway between illness and health. What is so disconcerting, she adds, about old age is that "normally it is an abnormal condition" (423).

Nobody likes being called old, the writer reminds us, and she proceeds to describe the shock we sense at meeting friends we have not seen for some years, a mutual shock indeed. One of the most revealing points is made by the essayist when she observes that "usually the subject profits by the distance that separates the in-itself from the for-itself in order to claim that ever-lasting youth their unconscious longs for" (435). Only a few old people questioned in a particular investigation thought they were old. Most felt younger than their age. In another circumstance, a woman living in an old age home said: "I don't feel at all old; sometimes I help the grannies, and then I say to myself, 'But you're a granny too' " (435). The author comments: "Confronted with the other old women, her immediate reaction was to think of herself as ageless: it required an effort of reflection for her to liken her situation to theirs" (435–36).

One of the reasons why Beauvoir's essay was hailed as a contribution to the knowledge about old age and a step toward correction of some of the wrongs done to old people is her boundless empathy, her understanding of frailties in human beings. Although critics, even before the publication of this book, had pointed to Beauvoir's preoccupation with death, with ageing, with many of the "scandals" in social life, it appears clearly from the pages of her sturdy essay that the main reason for the writing was the wish to clear the air of misunderstandings and to help correct attitudes based on prejudice. The empathy is felt with particular acuity in a passage where the author describes the increasing physical difficulties encountered by ageing people; the gradual or sometimes sudden loss of faculties, the diminishing strength and resourcefulness:

Even if the elderly person bears his ailments with resignation, they come between him and the world: they are the price he pays for most of the things he does. So he can no longer yield to a sudden desire or follow his whims: he ponders the consequences and he finds that he is forced to make a choice. If he goes for a walk to take advantage of a fine day, his feet will hurt him when he comes home; if he has a bath, his arthritis will torment him. He often needs help to walk or to wash, dress and so on; he hesitates to ask for it, preferring to do without. The level of inimicality in things rises: stairs are harder to climb, distances longer to travel, streets more dangerous to cross, parcels heavier to carry. The world is filled with traps; it bristles with threats. The old person may no longer stroll casually about in it. Every moment difficulties arise, and any mistake is severely punished. He needs artificial assistance to carry out his natural functions—false teeth, spectacles, hearing aids, walking sticks. . . . The sad part of it is that most old people are too poor to be able to afford good spectacles or hearing aids . . . and they are therefore condemned to half-blindness and total deafness. Shut in upon themselves, they fall into an inanition that diverts them from their struggle against their decline. A partial failure often brings about a renunciation that is followed by a rapid and general collapse. (451–52)

XIX   "It Is I Who Am Buried . . . "

With precision, yet with firm, delicate words, Beauvoir analyzes the complexities of sexual relations. Noting the persistence of the sex drive in most individuals, she finds simple and forceful formulations for the situation of loving couples and their problems. "In a couple whose love does away with the distance between the I and the other, even failure is overcome" (473), she writes. The old person, according to the essayist, often desires to desire because he retains his longing for experiences that can never be replaced and because "he is still attached to the erotic world he built up in his youth or maturity" (474). A fair amount of evidence is available, in Beauvoir's words, upon elderly men's sexual life. "It depends on their past and also upon their attitude towards their old age as a whole and towards their image in particular" (487).

Using examples drawn from the world of arts and letters, illustrations of a great many different experiences are given. Beauvoir wonders out aloud whether, as so many men in particular wished, the end of the sexual drive is a blessing or rather a diminution of the self, "a mutilation," an impoverishment. She sees a link between sexuality and creativity as in the cases of Victor Hugo and Picasso, among others.

While most passions tend to cool off with age, there is one that gets inflamed with age, jealousy. Beauvoir devotes considerable space to illustrations of this passion, notably through the examples of Juliette Drouet and Sophie Tolstoy. It would seem, though, that while the intensity of jealous feelings may become increased with age, this is not a passion exclusively reserved to that generation.

Chapter six, "Time, Activity, History," starts with a definition of the aged man as "an individual with a long existence behind him, and before him a very limited expectation of life" (536). Age changes our relationship with time, the author says: "As the years go by the future shortens while our past grows heavier" (542). Memory is what links us to the past, and in many people it is a powerful agent to help us relive stretches of our lives. Yet, the author warns us, memory can affect us negatively, too, and we must not expect to ever truly recapture any portion of our past: "The past moves us for the very reason that it is the past; but this too is why it so often disappoints us—we lived it in the present, a present rich in the future towards which it was hurrying; and all that is left is a skeleton. That is what makes pilgrimages so pointless" (543).

In a very moving page, Beauvoir evokes certain moments of grief that had seemed firmly anchored in her memory:

When Zaza died, I was too intent upon the future to weep for my own past. But I remember my distress, much later, at the death of Dullin, although indeed he and I had never been really intimate. It was a whole section of my life that collapsed: Ferolles, the Atelier, the rehearsals of *Les Mouches* and those wonderfully gay dinners when he used to tell his reminiscences—all these disappeared with him. Later our agreements and disagreements with Camus were wiped out: wiped out too my arguments with Merleau-Ponty . . . gone those long talks with Giacometti and my visits to his studio. So long as they were alive memory was not called upon for our shared past to remain alive in them. They have carried it away with them into the grave; and my memory can recover only a frigid imitation of it. In the "monuments to the dead" that stud my history, it is I who am buried. (545–46)

This testimonial reads like a page out of Simone de Beauvoir's own novel, *Tous les Hommes sont mortels (All Men Are Mortal)*. Like Fosca, her sadly immortal hero, she was left behind to testify to the friendship of those departed. But unlike Fosca, she lives her life consciously, actively, accepting her human, mortal condition courageously, and old age coming with it, too.

One may learn something positive from the ontological precision with which, in Beauvoir's operation, the future fuses into the past by the process of living, by way of the present. One may disagree with her on another contention: "No man can say, 'I have had a fine life,' because a life is something that one does not *have*, that one does not possess" (547). The disagreement would be more than mere semantics, to be sure, as each existent is entitled to his or her own view on the way life is lived.

Searching for explanations why, in their memories, old people so readily return to their childhood, the essayist comes up with an explanation that may satisfy, on psychological grounds: "The reason why they turn back so readily to their childhood is clear—they are possessed by it. Since it has never ceased to dwell in them, they recognize themselves in their childhood, even though for a while they may have chosen to ignore it . . . " (553). This is not, of course, the first and only time that Simone de Beauvoir insisted on the importance of childhood, especially early childhood, for the explanation of all our lives. She had said as much in several essays and in her memoirs as well.

After all the negative aspects of old age, the weaknesses and troubles, have been listed, though with deep understanding, and mercifully, one positive valorization occurs that deserves attention:

there is one form of experience that belongs only to those who are old—that of old age itself. The young have only vague and erroneous notions of it. One must have lived a long time to have a true idea of the human condition, and to have a broad view of the way in which things happen: it is only then that one can "foresee the present"—the task of the statesman. That is why, in the course of history, elderly men have been entrusted with great responsibilities. (567)

XX *Creativity in Old Age*

Setting out to finish her study of the relationship between the elderly man and his praxis by considering the old age of a few politicians, the author shows their variegated reactions to the realization of ageing. Some, she notes, go so far as to say they would be spared all regrets if they knew that the whole world would vanish with them. This cynical attitude spurs the essayist to voice a forceful credo to the contrary:

> There are others, and I am one of them, who are horrified by this idea. Like everybody else, I am incapable of conceiving infinity; and yet I do not accept finity. I want this adventure that is the context of my life to go on without end. I love young people: I want our species to go on in them and I want them to have a better life. Without this hope, I should find the old age towards which I am moving utterly unbearable. (613)

This is clearly a noble thought even though it is not without some fallacious implications and a flat contradiction of earlier views: the author had reminded us often enough that today's youth is tomorrow's old age. But it would be narrow-minded to hold her to a literal interpretation of her statements all the time. Her generosity is based on her own sense of responsibility and of duty to mankind. It is heartening to see she never once deviates from these goals.

Among the politicians discussed by Simone de Beauvoir, most experienced bitter disappointments in their last years over changes that went against the whole thrust of their lives' work. Churchill was thus disillusioned, and Gandhi even more so. The example of Clemenceau offers a typical evolution that demonstrates the gap between generations most vividly: "Clemenceau [illustrates that] . . . an elderly man who obstinately clings to his former position finds himself out of step with the present. Clemenceau's 'socialism' had become so out of date that it had turned into a policy of reaction" (628).

From an abstract fate, death, to the old person, becomes an event that is near at hand. As life grows less and less bearable on account of the various miseries of old age, death loses its fearful aspect and becomes more acceptable in many cases. One of the elements that bring about such a development is the impossibility of planning ahead, of making projects. As activities ebb, more people resign themselves to the inevitable. The author herself, feeling less regret

at the prospect of death, finds that the loss of friends and close
persons makes one's own absence from the world more bearable:

the idea of death saddens less than it did in former times: death is absence
from the world, and it was that absence that I could not resign myself to.
But by now so many absences have torn their gaps in me! My past is absent;
absent are my friends who have died and those I have lost; absent too so
many places in the world to which I shall never return again. When total
absence has swallowed everything, it will not make so great a difference.
(661–62)

XXI *Memory as an Ally*

Chapter seven discusses "Old Age and everyday Life." No matter
how diminished the old person may be, he continues nevertheless
to be what he was, according to the writer. It is the concern with the
past that helps him to live, and memory becomes the invaluable ally
in this endeavor. Old people show growing indifference and a lack of
curiosity toward the present. In some cases, the author notes,
strong ambition seizes the old one, as in the instance of Marshal
Pétain. In general, though, biological deterioration brings with it an
increasing detachment from the world.

Among the negative traits observed in high old age is growing
distrust, which, according to Beauvoir, is "the figurative expression
of the dependence" (692) in which they live. Habits become more
rigidly adhered to. Avarice develops, even in people who used to be
generous all their lives. The author relates this to the importance of
habit: an attachment to one's possessions derives from habit. Own-
ership, she finds, is a guarantee "of ontological security: the posses-
sor is his possession's reason for existence" (698). She points to the
pleasure people, especially old people, take in gazing at their possessions. "By means of what I possess, I recover an object that the
outside world may assimilate to my being, so that it is therefore not
for the outside world to decide who I am. Thanks to his possessions,
the old person assures himself of his identity against those who claim
to see him as nothing but an object" (699).

There is a certain degree of competition among old people in
social situations that bring them together or even in the absence of
such contact. Self-centeredness and indifference characterize many
old people. In a sad but plausible formula, the author shows the

causality of degradation in the aged: "Decline and distrust beget not only insensitivity with regard to others in the old person, but also hostility" (709). No wonder old people often act as prophets of doom. All these attitudes must irritate younger people, but, the author reminds us, we should understand the old: "Forgotten and treated with disrespect by the new generation," the elderly are challenging their judges "both now and in the future" (713).

There are a host of differing opinions about old age. What some observers call "shamelessness" may be just a form of liberation, especially in older women who want to assert themselves after a life of conformity. That liberation took on different forms for men as distinct from one another as Voltaire, Dr. Spock, Malesherbes—who defied his judges and showed complete fearlessness in the face of impending death—Bertrand Russell, and Pope John XXIII.

The eighth and last chapter proposes "Some Examples of Old Age." Here the writer assembles a few remarkable cases of vitality and creativity that stand out among the many old people who kept being active late in their lives. Victor Hugo's poetry written in his seventies proves to be a "remarkably young poetry," and yet it is one that is marked by age, Beauvoir maintains. Michelangelo, too, had an active and fruitful old age, though his work was hampered through all sorts of intrigues. Verdi's old age was one of amazing inventiveness; he celebrated triumphs, yet was always diffident and skeptical. Freud, despite enormous physical suffering and many successive operations for cancer, kept his mental abilities to the last.

Some of Beauvoir's illustrations, though instructive in various ways, add little in the way of proof: the pages on Chateaubriand and Lamartine, while of critical, biographical, and psychological interest, are a bit disappointing. Nothing essential is added to the author's thesis. On the other hand, one might have expected that more of the really striking cases of vigor at an advanced age, such as in a number of conductors in the twentieth century, would have been discussed. True, the essayist mentioned Casals, but there are any number of others, and it seems regrettable that this whole category of splendid maestros should have been omitted. Also, another whole class of people is missing: the many great minds who at an advanced age did things diametrically opposed to their whole life's work, as, for example, Knut Hamsun. But it would be idle to quibble about omissions and inclusions in a work as rich and instructive as this: out of an immense wealth of documentation, the essayist abstracted cases that suited her aim and added weight to her theory about old age.

XXII   A Conclusion That Actually Concludes

After completing this full and lively essay on old age, it would have sufficed for the author to write a perfunctory kind of ending. That is not what she chose to do. Her conclusion opens up more stimulating vistas on the whole complex of ageing and of death. Almost every line of what she writes here deserves mention. For brevity's sake, only the merest highlights will be singled out. "Old age is not a necessary end to human life," Beauvoir declares. "It does not even represent what Sartre called the 'necessity of our contingency,' as the body does" (800).

Reviewing the various ways in which civilizations dealt with old age, the author notes that the "vast majority of mankind look upon the coming of age with sorrow and rebellion. It fills them with more aversion than death itself" (800–801). Rightly, the essayist claims that the age at which decline begins depends upon the class to which one belongs:

Today a miner is finished, done for at the age of fifty, whereas many of the privileged carry their eighty years lightly. The workers' decline begins earlier; its course is also far more rapid. During his years of "survival" his shattered body is the victim of disease and infirmity; whereas an elderly man who has had the good fortune of being able to look after his health may keep it more or less undamaged until his death. (803)

The essayist's indictment of society is severe. As she had said earlier, it is the total picture of that society that is at fault with its inequities, its crass disregard of responsibilities and commitments. So her conclusion is not astonishing in its bitter tone:

That is the crime of our society. Its "old age policy" is scandalous. But even more scandalous still is the treatment that it inflicts upon the majority of men during their youth and their maturity. It prefabricates the maimed and wretched state that is theirs . . . when they are old. It is the fault of society that the decline of old age begins too early, that it is rapid, physically painful and, because they enter upon it with empty hands, morally atrocious. Some exploited, alienated individuals inevitably become "throwouts," "rejects," once their strength has failed them. (804–805)

The demands which the author formulates flow logically enough from this exposé. Seeing that society turns away from the aged worker "as though he belonged to another species," she writes: "That is why the whole question is buried in a conspiracy of silence. Old age exposes the failure of our entire civilization. It is the whole man that must be remade, it is the whole relationship between man and man that must be recast if we wish the old person's state to be acceptable" (806).

One would wish to be able to disagree with Beauvoir, but it cannot be denied that the question of old age is inseparable from the problem of equity and justice for all in social matters. Therefore, her concluding words ring true in their appeal to our conscience and to the attention of those able to affect legislation and supervision: "Once we have understood what the state of the aged really is, we cannot satisfy ourselves with calling for a more generous 'old age policy,' higher pensions, decent housing and organized leisure. It is the whole system that is at issue and our claim cannot be otherwise than radical—change life itself" (807).[17]

Critics have been quick to accuse Beauvoir of partisanship and of lack of objectivity. However, if anything is clear from the pages of this book, it is that she started out with as unbiased a mind as one could expect. Naturally, she had already had ample reason to find fault with our society, ever since *The Second Sex*. It is also true that for many decades she had sought to identify with left-wing causes. Yet she kept free from narrow party politics and, except for her militancy on behalf of some extreme left-wing youth groups, had known how to preserve her political independence. Her findings are all the more eloquent as she herself seems to have found a balanced and serene view of old age and of death. Her advice will prove indispensable in any overhaul of the "system." Mere reform would not do, if we believe her, and her warning is sounded in earnest: society has the potential to change for the better. But time is of the essence.

CHAPTER 5

Fiction

T HE memoirs tell us how the very young student already attempted a number of novelistic writings, none of which have appeared in public, except in synopses in the memoirs. As seen in her published novels, life is filtered down into her characters. But while the models are often recognizable, the ideas and conduct of the characters are original. To look for a point-for-point likeness between live models and any of Simone de Beauvoir's protagonists is futile. Once she feels inspired, once the broad outlines are marked, the author spins on in a fashion all her own. Thus we may believe her when, being questioned, she responded that Anne, for example, in *The Mandarins*, reflected her own personality to an extent, but bore other traits as well. We are sure to follow her explanation that Henri, in the same novel, while superficially offering similarities with Camus, is an incarnation of many of the author's own feelings, tastes, and leanings.

The traces of autobiographical borrowings, however, are many and often clear-cut, as in the Lewis episode in *The Mandarins*. Autobiographical reflections and developments are scattered all over Beauvoir's fiction, with the possible exception of *All Men are Mortal*, where the moods are based on experience; the expression of regrets over grievous errors and missed opportunities is psychologically accurate, yet no obvious parallels exist between any of the characters and any one linked to the author's own life.

The use of models may at times appear an asset: one of the most recognizable characters on that score, Scriassine in *The Mandarins*, is not only given many of the most striking characteristics of Arthur Koestler; he acts and speaks in a manner that makes the association inescapable, perhaps the only one of Beauvoir's characters to be so marked and drawn so clearly. All the others bear their own earmarks, they evolve away from the model. Scriassine, on the con-

154

trary, bears not just a resemblance to Koestler, he shares his obsessions and mannerisms—in short, he looks like an exact replica.

Through Simone de Beauvoir's memoirs, we are told precisely "who is who" in her novels and are thus able to rediscover many of the same people that Sartre portrayed in *Les Chemins de la Liberté (The Roads to Freedom)*, published respectively in 1943, 1945, and 1949.[1] It would seem likely that such multiple use of the same models might lead to reduplicating. As a matter of fact, that is no more the case than in, let us say, the Impressionist painters' or the Fauvists' use of models they shared. Each artist, each writer casts his characters in entirely original molds, and if the actual people are at times identifiable, this only makes the figures more lifelike, at least in Simone de Beauvoir's fiction. The same process of observing live models for use in creative writing may be noted in *The Mandarins*, after the publication of which, again, some critics were playing subtle guessing games as to who was behind such or such a character. True, resemblances are to be found between the fictional characters in Beauvoir's novels and real people. But in *She Came to Stay*, for one, there is never a mere plaster cast of a human being. The fictional heroes are autonomous and show the novelist capable of evoking with fine plasticity the interplay of personalities.

A volume of critical essays entitled *The Novelist as Philosopher*,[2] explores what has been a fruitful field of literary analysis and criticism at all times, but particularly in our era, where the challenge of testimony confronts writers and other artists. In Beauvoir's case— and her earlier novels were among the works examined in this volume—the trained philosopher as novelist is likely to be scrutinized at every step as to the philosophical content of her fiction. Jean-Paul Sartre was explicit in using his plays to flesh out complex points of metaphysical argument. His fiction, too, especially in the beginning ("The Wall," in *Intimacy and Other Stories*, and *Nausea*), was used consciously to popularize philosophical ideas. Simone de Beauvoir, on the other hand, has no such clear-cut intentions; hers is bona fide fiction. (For the sake of simplicity, and also because the problems dealt with are closely akin to those in the novels published just before and after it, Beauvoir's only play will also be briefly analyzed in this chapter. Incidentally, this play, *Les Bouches inutiles*, is an exception to the stated rule: here, didacticism and philosophical intent predominate.)

To be sure, dialogue in her novels is sometimes a vehicle for ideas, as it has been ever since novels were written, from Cervantes to Camus. The nature of the social milieu she writes about makes it imperative for the author to expose the motivations of the idealists or pragmatists she paints, so the reader can understand the ideological underpinnings of those often disconcerting people. After the initial trial and error period, Beauvoir appears comfortable in the writing of fiction; yet she has not published a novel since 1967. More pressing social, political, and ideological preoccupations have claimed her strength and attention. In that sense, her fictional output is open to definitive assessment, although the novelist has not forsworn novel writing.

I   L'Invitée (She Came to Stay, 1943)

Her first novel to be published, She Came to Stay, is not, of course, her first attempt at literary expression. The journals are explicit on this subject. But her earlier ones were lacking in life experience, whereas the making of She Came to Stay, protracted over a long period of time, dwelt on real people: the flesh and blood animating those pages show that the writer used no artifice to conceal the identities of her models.

The plot of the novel is fairly simple, although it should be borne in mind that some essential ideas and facts as well as side plots resist summarizing, here as in other novels. Françoise, a writer, lives with Pierre Labrousse, a stage director. For reasons not altogether clear, on a whim rather than rationally, they decide to "adopt," that is, emancipate, a provincial girl, Xavière Pagès (a surname, incidentally, to be found in the author's memoirs). They plan to attract her to Paris and are ready to assume the responsibility of preparing her for admission to the higher artistic and intellectual circles. However, Xavière is lethargic and resists being educated, all the while demanding attention and affection. When Pierre becomes interested in her otherwise than as a disciple, Françoise tries not to be jealous. Pierre's infatuation is clearer and clearer, and eventually Françoise solves the dilemma of the proverbial triangle by opening the gas tap: killing Xavière, she felt, was the only recourse left to her.

This bare bones summary neglects the rich, captivating atmosphere of the novel, one of Beauvoir's best, if not the best. The wanton and pretentious tone of artists' talk is exquisitely captured, as is the aimlessness of intellectuals with their constricting coteries. The air is thick with bombastic pronouncements of "existential" questions. Yet, this novel is not—not yet—beholden to any existentialist doctrine.[3] The epigraph, however, gave the book a problematic tinge. Hegel's apodictic claim that "each conscience pursues the death of the other" sets the tone for a philosophic discussion on human responsibility and the role of the ego. The novel posited the "scandal" of the other's existence in simple terms, thereby opening a passionate public debate.[4]

To understand how the trio of the novel could function for such a long time, we must note the fascination that Xavière feels for Françoise. Though the disciple's inertia is discouraging to Françoise, the fictional writer patiently clings to her methods of humoring the waif so that she may yet follow the example set for her. Thus it comes as a surprise that Xavière "adores" Françoise. The triangle is viable only as long as the affection of each for the other two is roughly equal.

The most "existential" appraisal of the trio is given by Elisabeth, who sees it from the outside and whose view is far from benevolent. "Did they know everything was false?—Surely they knew."[5] In her desperate frenzy, Elisabeth nevertheless reads things into the triangle that are excessive and unjust. Thus she believes the trio possible only because Pierre sleeps with Xavière—which the reader knows to be untrue—and, she speculates, perhaps because the two women have a lesbian relationship.

If one wonders how Françoise could be so infinitely patient with Xavière, the answer is simply that Françoise desperately wanted to share Xavière's life, a strange attitude indeed, but one which mirrors essential claims of existentialism, namely that one is responsible for other people's existence.[6] In *She Came to Stay*, we encounter a felicitous use of point of view. Though the narrative is in the third person, the reader very soon notices the autobiographical nature of much that Françoise says and thinks. It is, more often than not, as if the story were told in the first person, a technique which Beauvoir was to use to excellent effect, alternately with third person narrative, in *The Mandarins*.

Simone de Beauvoir patterned her characters after life, and this device injects an element of freshness, of lightness of touch, into a heady situation. It saves the novel from becoming a plea for Nietzschean arrogance and supermanlike presumption. For all her seemingly unscrupulous egotism, Françoise goes through harrowing trials of conscience before her act, which, incidentally, occurs with such casualness that calling it a crime may appear exaggerated. It is, rather, an accident due to specious arguing over the right of the individual to make decisions affecting the lives of others.

Françoise, with all her perplexities and the heavy inheritance of her overrefined feelings, is a lovable creature. The author has given her enough independence to make her a viable, full-blooded woman; she has portrayed her as a thinker of depth and merit, yet no preacher, whereas Pierre, for whose affection and love the two women compete, despite his superior mind, is not without a tendency toward pontificating. Though unsure of himself, he is seen by the others as being always in command. This misjudgment on their part leads to certain clashes between their personalities. In the end, the reader knows Pierre will not disapprove of Françoise's act.

Pierre's status as completely independent and unaccountable must appear somewhat unbelievable. He enjoys almost complete impunity as regards his feminine conquests. As long as his own heart seems intact and unaffected by his adventures, nothing troubles Françoise. It is only when the relations between him and Xavière are getting complicated that Françoise grows jealous. In retrospect, the sexual carte blanche that Pierre received from Françoise is less than fully plausible. Thus we are shown Pierre, with the genuine insensitivity of egotists, asking Françoise, barely recovered from serious illness, questions about Xavière that must make her suffer.

Compared to the depth of psychological insight which appears in *La Femme Rompue (The Woman Destroyed,* 1967), *She Came to Stay* shows the author still confined to mere theory. No deeply painful experience had yet marred her life. In that respect, the later novels of Simone de Beauvoir (from *The Mandarins,* published in 1954, to *Les Belles Images,* 1966, and *The Woman Destroyed)* display far more insight into the human heart. They also reveal a more pessimistic outlook on life.

The novelist is at her best in the description of emotional drama, as in the potentially awkward scene where Pierre eavesdrops on Xavière, who had locked herself with Gerbert in her room; in the evocation of late night ambience in a bar where Xavière performs the famous "acte gratuit" by burning a hole in the palm of her hand with a cigarette—a scene almost identical with Sartre's "acte gratuit" in *The Age of Reason,* where first Ivich and then Mathieu plunge a large knife into their hands.[7]

The fact that *She Came to Stay* bears the name of the very alive

Olga Kosakiewicz on the dedication page may reassure those who have been privileged to read the author's memoirs: Xavière may be dead at the end of the novel, but like an actress after the curtain has fallen on the murder of the heroine, she is to rise and bow. Philosophical murder lacks credibility, and this element is perhaps a weak point in an otherwise taut novel. The author readily concedes this.[8] In view of the use of real life models, as we are shown it through frank statements in the memoirs, it seems futile to hunt for exact correspondences in this novel between fictional characters and persons in the author's life. There is more than one trait in Pierre reminiscent of Sartre; Françoise shows fundamental similarities with the author herself as to ideas, tastes, and dislikes. Xavière is obviously patterned after Olga, often mentioned in the memoirs. Other figures, too, may evoke actual people, as will be the case even more intensely in *The Mandarins*. Above all, the atmosphere, saturated with cigarette smoke and with heavy drinking into the early morning hours, in bars and cafés, is a transposition of the author's own world into fiction. The characters, however, follow their own logic, free from any indebtedness to models.[9]

She Came to Stay is a sturdy novel, intellectually satisfying and with enough drama and suspense to keep a reader's interest. Through its publication, Simone de Beauvoir established her reputation in the literary world. Speaking of this novel in connection with a number of Sartre's, Camus', and Beauvoir's books, the late Gaëtan Picon found that what we are confronted with is a "literature of lucidity, and no longer of imagination. That lucidity, however, is not applied to psychology. The inventory of our conscience," he writes, "is succeeded by a description of man's situation in the world, of man's relation with the universe, with existence, with History, and with the other. . . ."[10] Picon's observation, pertinent to the whole of existentialist writing, is particularly apt and fitting for *She Came to Stay*.

II Le Sang des Autres (The Blood of Others, 1945)

Instead of progress, this second novel to a certain extent represents a regression. The problem that is proposed by Beauvoir is in itself a fascinating illustration of a major existentialist tenet: responsibility arises not so much out of our acts and their consequences as from the mere fact of our existence. "Chacun est responsable de tout" ("everyone is responsible for everything").[11]

The novel is in the form of a long discourse pondering that thesis. The hero, Jean Blomart, has to decide before dawn whether the Resistance group whose leader he is should continue its acts of sabotage, and thereby risk provoking reprisals by the Germans against the civilian population. Thinking back on his past, he begins to realize that by each of his earlier major decisions, he somehow caused suffering to those closest to him. Thus he alienated his mother when he joined the Communist party, breaking with his own class—a dilemma that Blomart shares with Hugo in Sartre's play *Les Mains Sales* (Dirty Hands, 1948), who bears other traits similar to him.

Jean caused the death of his best friend, Jacques, by dragging him into a demonstration that turned violent. He also allowed his fiancee, Hélène, to leave on a dangerous Resistance mission, whence she returned fatally injured. Jean's guilt in the ruin of those dear to him is ever-present to him. Watching Hélène draw close to her end, he discovers that each *existant* is responsible for others just as for himself, that he is tied inextricably to the world and to others no matter what he does.[12]

The narrative, which alternates between the "I" form and the third person, à la John Dos Passos, amalgamating historicity and fiction, is often stilted. The stylization of history comes off least well.[13] Yet, there are scenes of genuine immediacy. Jean, retracing his steps into a past which weighs on him, feels the "curse of being another"[14] as an "injustice" that hurts him far more deeply than his friend Paul's rancor. Comparing his own with the involvement of his associates, he finds that, on balance, his own commitment is wanting: "Gauthier était pacifiste. Paul était communiste. Hélène était amoureuse. Laurent était un ouvrier. Et moi je n'étais rien. . . ."[15] In trying to find an explanation for his frustration, he does not accept Paul's hint that if, indeed, he, Jean, was nothing at all, it was because he was neither a bourgeois nor a worker. Jean thinks that "rather I was neither bourgeois nor worker because I could not be anything: neither bourgeois nor worker; neither a pacifist nor a hawk; neither loving nor indifferent. . . ."[16]

Simone de Beauvoir recognized the artificiality of what she had written. In the second volume of her memoirs, she noted:

rereading the novel today, what strikes me is how lacking my characters were in relief, in reality . . . they are defined by moral attitudes whose roots

I never sought to grasp. I attributed to Blomart some of the emotions of my childhood. Those would not justify the guilt feeling that weighs down his whole life. I realized that to some extent and I imagined that at twenty he had caused the death of his best friend. But an accident never suffices to determine a whole existence. Later on, Blomart is conforming too much to the conduct I assigned him. I did not yet know anything about trade unions and their struggles. The fictional world in which I involved my characters does not have the complexity it should have had for an authentic *militant*. The relief, the experience which I endowed him with are abstract constructions and lack truth. Hélène has more life blood—I gave her more of my own traits. The chapters written from her viewpoint displease me less.[17]

While the author thus keeps her distance from a work that had a mixed reception, critics have expressed varied views on *The Blood of Others*. Noting how original *She Came to Stay* had been, how gifted and hard-headed Beauvoir proved in her first novel, Maurice Nadeau wrote that neither *The Blood of Others* nor *All Men are Mortal* is based on the same genuine lived and living experience[18] and show the philosophic ficelles clearly. Generalizing his findings on existentialist novelists, Nadeau states: "Existentialist novelists want to write 'significant' works—'des oeuvres signifiantes', to use the philosophic jargon. In the hands of the less gifted ones, the novel is becoming a more or less well-ordained ballet of philosophical, moral, even sociological concepts."[19]

And Gaëtan Picon, viewing existentialist writings in general, wrote: "It would not be accurate to say that Sartre or Camus or Simone de Beauvoir writes novels only in order to flesh out a preconceived image of man and a vista of things rationalized beforehand. But they write novels only inasmuch as they follow their philosophic thought. . . ."[20]

III   Les Bouches Inutiles (1945)

If such was the view expressed by leading French critics on Simone de Beauvoir's second novel, her only play, *Les Bouches Inutiles*, was precisely the illustration of a philosophical theory by a concrete situation. Although some of the scenes achieve a dramatic momentum, the play as a whole cannot sustain its message throughout and falls short of its goal. The author, with her usual candor, admits the main shortcomings: she describes in her memoirs how, casting about to find a suitable subject, she came across an old chronicle that filled the bill:

a city that had just overthrown a democratic regime found itself threatened by a despot. Then the question of means versus ends was to arise: has one the right to sacrifice individuals for the general future good? Partly to satisfy the needs of the plot, and partly through what was, at the time, my natural inclination, I slipped into a moralizing role.

I made the same mistake as in *The Blood of Others* (from which I also borrowed numerous leitmotivs): my characters became reduced to mere ethical viewpoints. The leading male character, Jean-Pierre, is another version of Jean Blomart: since he cannot formulate a code of conduct which does justice to all men, he opts for abstention. "How can you measure the weight of a tear against the weight of a drop of blood?" he asks. . . . The principle of evil (le Mal) is personified in . . . the Fascist Georges, and in the ambitious François Rosbourg: by their underhanded scheming they demonstrate that oppression is not something one *chooses* to take part in: from the moment it creeps into society it rots it throughout. The means are inseparable from the envisaged end, and if the two come into conflict, it is the end which is perverted . . . .

My condemnation of this play is not without certain reservations. In the first half, the dialogue has a certain power, and some passages produce a fine effect of dramatic suspense. It was daring of me to try and put an entire town on the stage but this audacity can be defended on the grounds that at the time we were, quite fortuitously, living at the height of a critical period of history. As for the denouement, it is no worse and no better than any other. My mistake was to pose a political problem in terms of abstract morality. . . .[21]

The author's retrospective opinion was given at this length to show the distance gained by her. At the same time, her favorable view of portions of her play was shared by not a few of her critics, including the most demanding ones, who, like Pierre de Boisdeffre, reluctantly acknowledged the merits of an otherwise unsuccessful play. The philosophical point made in this play uses a grossly exaggerated sense of patriotism which makes it necessary, in order to hold the city, to sacrifice its "useless mouths"—a claim tragically and prophetically like the pronouncement of an American military officer who during the Vietnam war declared: "It was necessary to destroy the town in order to save it." The "useless mouths"—the women, the old people, the children—are the very elements whose safeguard genuine patriotism must insure.

If Beauvoir's sagacity was not at fault, her dramatic skill was inadequate. The actual plot picks up the situation provided by the chronicle, actually combined by the author from an Italian source transposed to Flanders, which, she contends, knew similar conflicts: the town of Vauxcelles, under siege by the Burgundians, learns from a messenger who was able to slip through the enemy lines that the king of France will send relief through his armies only in the spring. The reserves of food will not allow the population to survive until then. That is why the council rules that "useless mouths" will be relegated onto the outer moat, to starve to death. The messenger, who had been invited to share the responsibility, at first refuses to become a party to the forced exile of the weak. Eventually, however, he accepts the offer, using his share of power to decide a desperate *sortie* which can end only in victory or death. At the conclusion of the play, the gates are opened.

Retrospectively, Beauvoir records that "the idealism which permeates the play is now bothering me and I deplore its didacticism. . . . "22

IV   Tous les Hommes sont mortels (All Men Are Mortal, *1947*)

At times, it may be possible to forget that Simone de Beauvoir the novelist started out as a philosopher. Her drive and impetus in the final version of *She Came to Stay* as well as in *The Mandarins* succeeded in overshadowing the purely philosophical problems. But in her third novel, we never once are allowed to forget the philosopher behind the novelist. And yet, although the whole novel revolves around a narrowly defined thesis—mortality is better than immortality—there are long moments of drama, of genuine poignancy that bring to the fore all that is human, drowning out mere theory.

If we grant the author that immortality may be achieved by magic means, the plot of this novel becomes credible. Its fifteenth century hero, Fosca, is the prince of a North Italian city state, Carmona, which affords but limited possibilities for action to his boundless ambition. He accepts the challenge of becoming immortal by drinking a potion insuring eternal life, mainly to find new outlets for his ambitions. Henceforth, he takes part in the shaping of history on a worldwide scale. At the outset, he labored to enhance the status of his native city, Carmona. Yet, unwittingly, he helped the king of France's policy. Fosca flees to Austria, becoming the advisor to Charles the Fifth. He witnesses the formation of the league of German states, the expedition of Columbus; he accompanies Jacques Cartier to America, discovering vast new territories. We see him

further on in the entourage of eighteenth century *philosophes;* later
yet, he becomes a participant in the revolution of 1848.

His friends die one after the other; so do the women attracted to
him, and Fosca feels further and further removed from humanity.
As one reads of ageless, unending life, one becomes more acutely
aware of the futility of thought and language which reflects our fast,
superficial lives. Small wonder if Fosca, living through the ceaseless
unfolding of history, has grown indifferent to the fate of mortals,
which is to die too soon to discover the meaning of life. He is no
longer able to hold on to human affairs; his love for successive
women dries up.

"Fosca's immortality becomes damnation pure and simple," says
one of the author's biographers and critics, adding: "Through this
dream of unachievable immortality what is also implied is the myth
of mankind finally unified which Hegel bestowed on Marxism."[23]

On a less exalted level, other critics found the novel wanting.
Thus, Frances Keene finds the mere display of historical research,
unallayed by a consistently gripping sequence of human interest,
trying for the reader's attention. She further reminds us that Virginia Woolf's *Orlando* had attempted an even bolder thrust into
immortality, "making it a living work of art." She feels that Simone
de Beauvoir fails "because Mlle de Beauvoir's heart is just not in
it."[24]

As so often with Beauvoir's books, critics are divided as to the
merits of *All Men are Mortal*. While a majority, giving faint praise to
the author's graceful attempt at creating a fictional speculation on a
philosophical theme, do not value the novel highly, some find it
delightful. Maurice Cranston, writing on Beauvoir in *The Novelist
as Philosopher*, calls it "one of her most successful novels" and at
one time compares the author to David Hume as a writer of
paraboles.[25]

V   Les Mandarins (The Mandarins, 1954)

Many readers have called this novel, Beauvoir's most successful and the occasion for a Prix Goncourt, a roman à clef. Because
several characters are verifiably similar to real people, it was
claimed that the whole plot must be close to events and personalities of real life. The author staunchly refutes such an interpretation. The atmosphere in the novel, however, is truthful to the
Paris of 1944–1947.

Henri Perron, a journalist and playwright, directs *L'Espoir*, a newspaper voicing strong support for idealistic democracy; its left-wing orientation is eventually tempered by the vigorous reaction to news of Soviet forced labor camps. Perron's friend Robert Dubreuilh, while also affected by the sobering revelations on Soviet camp conditions, long favors a discipline of the left that would overlook certain blemishes on the ideal. His wife, Anne, a psychiatrist, for a time tries to mediate between the two friends, who eventually break over Dubreuilh's rather reckless tactics in making *L'Espoir* available to a group of politicians unpalatable to the director, who resigns and reverts to free-lance writing.

Most of the numerous secondary characters, strongly individual, present their political and philosophical conflicts through lively dialogues. They are often seen through acts of violence, explained as an aftereffect of the clandestine struggle against the Nazi occupation. The "Mandarins" are the intellectual leaders, shown to be helplessly engaged in a game of politics too complicated for them, a game from which they can extricate themselves only through painful sacrifices. The psychological truthfulness of this fresco of postwar France, particularly Paris, is recognized by many, even among the author's sharpest critics. What is best in this novel is the impression of fermentation in many circles, of vehement confrontation between the different groups within the left wing, and of the often cynical attempts by former collaborationists to profit from the confusion among idealistic young people in search of an ideological identity.

Without judging the various viewpoints, yet endowing the conflicting debaters with wholesome arguments, the author vividly conveys the bubbling life of the late forties as she experienced it herself in those years. We know from the memoirs that the characters in *The Mandarins* bear traits from people she had known and observed. While the protagonists have many features that seem readily recognizable, their conduct and their reasoning make them genuinely independent, original figures. Thus, Perron resembles Camus in many respects, but he also has traits of the author herself.

Dubreuilh has been compared to Jean-Paul Sartre, but this robs the model as well as the fictional hero of his complexity. At any rate, the character in the novel acts and speaks generally in ways alien to the model's, even though, occasionally, he does voice opinions in line with Sartre's. He leads a life all his own.

The same observation holds true for Lewis Brogan, Anne's

American lover, though it is regrettable that the book's dedication to
Nelson Algren seems to authorize a complete equation with the
American novelist. That, however, is only a matter of the author's
lack of discretion, not lack of imagination. Lewis becomes a full-
fledged partner to Anne's dream fulfillment when they first meet
and cautiously fall in love, despite all warnings on either side, and
again when they travel to Central America in one of the finest
sequences of a novel filled with the tensions of active lives.

Grown more discerning and less of an exhibitionist, when
Beauvoir writes about the episode of her life years later in her
memoirs, she gives us a sober portrait of Nelson Algren that allows
us to put in perspective the clashes of personalities and ideas depicted in the novel. The memoirs also serve as a clarifying agent,
since incidents in the novel that are reminiscent of real life events
are told in the memoirs stripped of the passion that frequently
overlays the novelistic narrative. The writer indeed portrayed all
her characters from a considerable distance, even those most closely
resembling her own disposition, such as Anne and Henri.

Besides the political and ideological plot, there are sentimental
involvements. The more central of these concern Henri, who, however half-heartedly or listlessly, continuously tries to break with his
beautiful but neurotic mistress, Paula. In the opening part of the
book, Henri is aggressively pursued by Nadine, Anne Dubreuilh's
daughter, who challenges Henri to take her with him on his first,
long-coveted post-liberation trip to Portugal. When they return,
Henri tries unsuccessfully to shake off the cumbersome relationship. Through a long array of casual affairs, resulting in part from
this rebuff, Nadine eventually outgrows her naive penchant for lost
causes and their heroes to become a sane member of society whom
Henri will be proud to marry.

Anne in her sentimental evolution goes from a quietly happy and
fulfilled professional wife, through passionate attachment to Lewis,
to the resignation that her inability to choose between Robert and
Lewis has made inevitable. Equally fond of both men, she turns
toward a deeper involvement in her chosen profession to overcome
the bitter feeling of loss caused by her own indecision. Although
Beauvoir strives valiantly to make that evolution believable, it is not
the best part of an otherwise taut and lively novel.

There are a few flaws, most of them in the presentation of very minor characters. At one time there is a factual contradiction of the type the *New Yorker* categorizes as "our forgetful authors."[26] Again, as so often in Beauvoir's books, the style tends to be lax, even though this book has been remarkably well revised and thus avoids most of her usual boners.

In the turmoil of Parisian intellectual and political life which forms the background of the novel, there are few areas of calm, reflective life. Dubreuilh is an oasis of peaceful, serene domination, and this may be an offshoot of the author's admiration for Sartre, the main model for this character. Dubreuilh is endowed with almost superhuman patience and an unfailing sense of humor that enable him to weather the political and personal storms besieging his life. In fact, he is almost too good to be believable, whereas Anne is shown to be tormented by many doubts. Her often impulsive reaction to crises or dilemmas makes her painfully human, so that her occasional omniscience becomes bearable. Having chosen psychiatry as Anne's profession, the author found herself mandated to prove Anne's mental, moral, and intellectual stability. Anne comes out of her trials with poise and relatively unruffled, even when it is a matter of coping with her daughter's eccentricities. It is only when she herself is deeply involved that her professionalism forsakes her. This feature makes Anne frail and fallible, a much more credible human being. For a novelist of so robust a constitution as Beauvoir, this is no mean accomplishment. It contributes signally to the merit of *The Mandarins*.

Another part of her projected ego—if one may say so—is to be found in Henri. Admired by his young reporters and other associates, Henri, the outspoken advocate of a staunch liberal line, is deeply divided between the demanding certainties of opinion and belief, on the one hand, and the temptation to yield to the facile triumph of his intellectual and physical assets. His attitude toward Paula is awkward and lacks spontaneity and sincerity. Had he had the courage to break frankly, he might not have had the nagging sense of guilt throughout various infatuations and whimsical adventures. As things drag on, Henri feels estranged from the woman he had loved and who had given him the best of herself.

Thanks to a passage in the second volume of Beauvoir's memoirs, we now know that Paula was patterned after a real life model whose pathetic story does not, however, have the relatively happy ending

the author granted Paula's. The fictional character has the same
degree of intensity, even of frenzy, as the real woman had shown,
without, however, bearing the same pathological traits.[27]

In the novel, when she wastes her talents as a singer because she
no longer has any ambition except to please Henri, Paula grows into
an idle, passive drone whose very existence is a living reproach to
Henri. Since he no longer wants her, but lacks the courage to tell
her so, every word Paula says aggravates him, every gesture, to
him, underlines the ever-increasing distance between them, which
she alone does not feel. It is only after protracted suffering, caused
by her refusal to believe in the obvious estrangement, that Paula is
cured of her single passion, Henri. However, the cure appears
worse than the disease, for after she realizes the gap between them,
she is no longer secure in any respect, and her attempt at asserting
herself, at regaining her mental balance—making believe she had
overcome the crisis—shows her oddly removed from reality, despite
all her efforts to appear up to date, "à la page," and "with it." She
remains a beautiful empty shell, pitied by Anne, who is her only
true friend.

Henri, who always was dead set against compromise in politics,
whose principles seemed rigidly adhered to, and who had proven by
his courageous acts during the Occupation that he valued freedom,
justice, and decency above all else and was not afraid of dying for
them—Henri precisely is doomed to compromise and to act un-
scrupulously. This appears mainly in his involvement with
Josette—a beautiful though stained young woman who is manipu-
lated by her collaborationist mother—but also in large part in his
friendships with various individuals and groups of people. Ultimately he will conquer these weaknesses, and the denouement is
optimistic: out of his trial by fire, Henri emerges unscathed, his
friendship with Dubreuilh solidly renewed; he is confident in the
future, in a life of fulfillment and shared responsibility. His daughter
by Nadine will know a better world.

The optimism of this conclusion is not universal. Anne no longer
expects anything from life; when everybody around her is happy,
active, and busy changing the world, she alone is sad. Even Henri,
while sharing the relief and happiness at the recovery of freedom
from private and political nightmares, remains thoughtful and
melancholy as he thinks back to that first Christmas after the Lib-

eration when the world looked so rosy, when every hope was permissible:

> They had been laughing happily together, congratulating each other on the victory, shouting "Long live America" . . . and drinking to the Soviet Union. And Sezenac was a traitor, helpful America was preparing to subjugate Europe, and as for what was going on in Russia, it was better not to look too closely. Emptied of the promises it had never held, the past was nothing but a booby trap. . . .[28]

Henri's mournful look backwards is, of course, yet another expression of the author's own divided mind. Confident in progress on the one hand, while remaining an activist through the age-old scepticism which she always shared with Sartre, Beauvoir is indeed one of those "Mandarins" whom she described.

Dubreuilh, whose wisdom and patience had helped Anne overcome many a crisis in the difficult process of ageing, shows one more characteristic linking him to Sartre when he remarks to his wife: "One book more or less isn't very important."[29] Those are the words Anne remembers from the discussion she had with her husband a while earlier. What Dubreuilh actually said was: "one book more or less on earth isn't as important as all that. . . ."[30] The reader will notice that this opinion faithfully reflects a permanent trend in Sartre's outlook on life, as he voiced it in an interview with *Le Nouvel Observateur* in the late sixties: "*Nausea* is of no value when it comes to comparing a book to the very real suffering of a hungry child. . . ."[31] It is not surprising that Beauvoir should have captured Sartre's predominant mood, that of a real humanist—a word, incidentally, that makes Sartre shudder or snicker, according to his disposition, shared by Beauvoir; his refusal to accept the Nobel Prize for Literature stems from just such an attitude toward what he considered soft thought as opposed to the hard thought of logic. What is admirable is that his lifelong companion, who fully shared his views in this respect, succeeded in introducing into her novel elements of social conscience that prevail over the natural egotism of her protagonists.

Replying to Scriassine's question about the conditions of life under the Occupation, Anne feels inadequate to that task: "I tried hard to give a satisfactory answer to his question but I succeeded rather poorly: everything had been either worse or more bearable than what he imagined."[32] Anne's reticence is a typical reaction of one who had lived through the experience; words cannot convey an exact picture of what the day to day existence had been. Sartre, in one of his essays, gives a masterful explanation of those dark days: "We have never been freer than under the Occupation," one of the most beautifully true formulations of reality in his entire work.[33] That paradox, worded so succinctly by Sartre, illuminates the difficulty Anne feels in answering Scriassine.

While many passages in Beauvoir's writings lend themselves to criticism, especially on grounds of psychological implausibility, none of them offend the standards of morality current at the time her book appeared, let alone those of today. To maintain the contrary and to take exception to any situation in her novels as *scabreux*—slippery—a reproach dolefully formulated over and over again by hostile critics—is as ridiculous a charge as it is inane. It takes an unusual degree of *Tartufferie* to maintain that Beauvoir in any way corrupted public morality. The offense, here as so often, is strictly in the eye of the beholder.[34]

VI   Les Belles Images (1966)

One might read this novel from cover to cover without once remembering it was written by the author of *The Mandarins* and *The Second Sex*. The dialogue flows smoothly, a smoothness intended to convey the shallow, trite preoccupations of "in" people: hi-fis, cars, Christmas gifts, transatlantic vacations—the picture is successful as far as the great void of today's metropolitan scene is concerned. Parisian suburbia appears akin to its American counterpart: it has the same surface luxury, the same basic insecurity and glib social talk. Those "new" architects may all be alive; their problems may even be real. The clash of ideas, however, does not seem convincing.

Laurence, the heroine of the novel, finds all her associations and relationships lacking in authenticity. Her husband, her lover, even her father, whom she prefers to these, and her job—all are artificial. She works at inventing advertising slogans—the "beautiful images" of the title.

The focus of the novel is on personal problems. If the "beautiful pictures" appeared to be what the "idea girl," Laurence, contributes to the advertising agency's pool, we see later that every idea becomes deflated through being magnified like a balloon. Every thought in this practical realm, through an inescapable association of ideas, becomes something usable. The deeper we go into Laurence's life (and it is not very deep, actually), the better we are able to see that those "beautiful pictures" have taken over every aspect of her life, chasing authenticity away. Her final task will be to refuse being no more than a beautiful picture.

The passionate reaction of Laurence's mother upon hearing of her own lover's wish to break with her inevitably recalls a situation in *The Mandarins* where Paula refused to accept reality under similar circumstances. But unlike Paula, Dominique shows her claws: she sends off a letter of revelations to Gilbert's fiancée, thereby provoking Gilbert to act like the boorish brute he always was underneath all his charm. When Gilbert slaps Dominique, the humiliation sobers the aging woman, who finally allows her divorced husband to grow close to her again.

Such a summary shows nothing of the psychological structure of the novel. Yet the motivation of the characters is persuasive, in particular Laurence's. Far more than her mother, she is struggling with an uncomprehending environment. Her husband, Jean-Charles, seemed to fit into her life with near perfection. Still, when Laurence avoids hitting a cyclist, thereby damaging their car beyond repair, Jean-Charles cannot help bearing an obvious grudge against her. "Would you have killed the cyclist to save eight hundred thousand francs?" she asks in reply.[35]

They disagree on their children's education. While physically harmonious, the couple thus falls apart. There is a strong hint at Laurence's earlier nervous breakdown, when Jean-Charles was successful in patching over their differences stemming largely from Laurence's violent reaction upon hearing of torture used by the French in Algeria.

Lucien, her lover, is shown only fleetingly. Laurence had allowed herself to slide into this clandestine relationship without any strong reason. When Lucien showers her with reproaches, Laurence calmly breaks off the affair. In this particular scene, the author may deserve Mark Slonim's criticism that her characters are merely representations of ideas and rather lifeless.[36] Finally, Laurence's father, so profoundly admired by her, the only being who had seemed unselfish enough to take cognizance of her existence, proves to be disappointing; on their—quite unbelievable—trip to Greece, he raves about sights and monuments, while she feels cheated. There is no revelation of what his "secret" might be. Why was he so self-contained, why did he give such an overwhelming impression of contentment, of wisdom? The reader of Simone de Beauvoir's other novels and especially of her memoirs cannot help but find a parallel between the father and Jean-Paul Sartre, a parallel all the more astonishing as other characters in this novel are less clearly recognizable. Particularly, the two women bearing some possible traits of the author, Dominique and her daughter, Laurence, are miles away from Simone de Beauvoir in their tastes, opinions (except Laurence's on torture), and mannerisms.

In comparison to *The Mandarins*, *Les Belles Images* shows a paucity of ideas, even though inauthenticity and ageing are important themes. The novelist, however, does show growth in her portrayal of intimate relationships. Critics have taken Beauvoir to task, in *Les Belles Images* as well as in *The Mandarins*, for failing to convincingly depict the relationship between mothers and daughters. Because the author often stated her determination not to give birth, the critics, conveniently ignoring the reasons why the author never wanted children, have concluded that she must be ignorant about child psychology and motherly feelings altogether. That this is untrue is easily verifiable for any reader of *The Second Sex*, *A Very Easy Death*, and *The Coming of Age*.

To get back to the theme of *Les Belles Images*, those "images" are all the delusions of the upper middle class. In this novel, Beauvoir tried hard not to write in a "committed" way. Only occasionally is there a hint that this is the same writer who took sides so actively in other works. For example, the male chauvinist lawyer, Thirion, is a caricature of a die-hard reactionary; by comparison with him, the "feminist" husband of the heroine, Jean-Charles, seems forward looking.

Laurence herself felt traumatized through the shock she suffered when learning of torture in the French Vietnam and Algerian wars. But subsequently, in deference to her husband's dictates, she totally accepts abstaining from keeping informed. In a similar vein, she aims at preserving her ten year old daughter, Catherine, from being confronted with the ugly, painful side of life through newspapers or television—of course an impossible endeavor. For all these reasons, Laurence remains a somewhat less than fully satisfying heroine. Suffering deeply from the disillusionment of life, sensing her husband's diminishing affection, having to deal with a selfish lover along with a mother who never was close to her, and ultimately finding even her long venerated father wanting, she realized that these, too, were "images," just as a child was an image or she herself was seen to be one.

Though uneven, the novel does have some positive sides to it. The distinguished literary critic, Etienne Lalou, couched his findings in soothing terms when he called *Les Belles Images* a "relative failure," saying it is redeeming itself.

> A triumphant Simone de Beauvoir would have been an unbearable bluestocking. A Simone de Beauvoir struggling with heart-rending intelligence and sincerity with the contradictions of the human condition touches our hearts. That is why none of her works can be indifferent. Every one of them evokes our own intimate conflicts, bourgeois that we are, both proud and ashamed to be bourgeois . . . [37]

Less charitable, Charles Poore[38] sees nothing but frivolity in *Les Belles Images*. And, of course, even Lalou could not extend his charity to the many flaws in the book, although he reverts to praise:

> How could one remain insensitive to the purity and the sincerity of an art which, with the simplest of means, reconciles the two opposite poles of Simone de Beauvoir's personality, an austere philosopher and a sentimental "midinette." From that synthesis is born an authentic novelist who is also a lucid yet moving moralist.[39]

The praise, by the way, resembles a cunningly disguised disparagement, for being called a *midinette* could not be pleasant to the novelist.

Literary criteria were not the only ones used in the various assessments of *Les Belles Images*. Ever since the author had published her manifesto on women's liberation, *The Second Sex*, critics, above all male critics, have suspected her of sneaking feminist propaganda into her novels. What the novelist may pursue in this particular case is an attempt to shore up evidence of the futility and frivolousness of women's professionalism without strong ideological commitment. The lives of both men and women in this novel are too stereotyped to convey a keen awareness of social problems. Somehow, the author got caught in her own net: for in trying to depict a scatterbrained society, she may have succeeded beyond her original goals.

Life seldom resembles the conditions portrayed in *Les Belles Images* save for the caricatural evocations that are on the whole successful, such as the people in the agency; Laurence's mother, Dominique; the figure of the husband, Jean-Charles, who despite some pleasant features is obtuse and conceited; Dominique's lover, Gilbert, and his high-sounding flippancy. In short, most of the society presented in *Les Belles Images* amounts to a caricatural outline of mankind. Even the tone of the narrative is kept on a level of persiflage: one wonders, at the beginning whether the name of the author on the cover of the book might not be Marguerite Duras, who occasionally resorts to the same kind of commonplace dialogue to describe unsophisticated people. Yet the conclusion the author offers is serious; caricature was used only to enhance the sense of pathetic futility found in the empty world of "images."

VII   "L'Age de Discretion" (The Age of Discretion, *1967*)

The woman writer who is narrating this story is married to André, a scientist, sixty-nine, who is as successful in his field as she has been to date in hers. Her latest book of essays, however, does not get a good critical reception, which is shattering to her. On top of that, their son Philippe, brought up to share their liberal, agnostic views but married to a rich girl, has accepted a high government post, thereby giving up an academic career, without telling his mother beforehand. She considers this not just wrong but an outright betrayal of all his past, his ideals. To this, the son retorts that there comes a point in life at which one must discover one's own values.

André is patterned in large part after Sartre. The mother (whose name is never revealed, while all the other characters have names) obviously has many traits of Simone de Beauvoir's own character. The only major flaw, to this reader, is in the mother-son relationship, which is hardly credible. Even a Spartan mother had more feeling for her own flesh and blood than this intellectual shrew, who condemns Philippe in the name of a principle. Her adamant refusal to see the son who wishes to make up with her bespeaks a rigidity totally uncharacteristic of the author. When Philippe returns to offer his apologies, he is tender and understanding; but faced with his mother's intransigence, he shouts "farewell" and leaves. The narrator's moroseness recalls the attitude of Xavière in *She Came to*

Stay more than that of any other of Beauvoir's characters. Grieving and pouting, the story's mother is bound to lose her son for good were it not for her husband's more realistic, more humane and open-minded outlook.

Some of the discreetly used autobiographical touches lend a note of genuineness to this otherwise essentially cerebral study of contrasts between generations. Thus, the narrator notes with regard to her husband's opinion of her writing: "He does not tell me so, but deep down he is quite sure that from now on I shall do nothing that will add to my reputation. . . . "[40] But she hastens to add—is it the fictional writer only?—"This does not worry me, because I know he is wrong. I have just written my best book, and the second volume will go even further."[41] Still—and this may be seen as an allusion to the author's own experience— the narrator notes: "When I was a child, when I was an adolescent, books saved me from despair . . . "[42]—which persuaded her that culture is the highest value in life.

If there had been any doubt in the reader's mind as to whether some of the feelings expressed or recorded in this story were related to the novelist's own life, no such doubt can survive the reading of what is a kind of variation on a theme coined by her concerning Sartre; André, moody and a bit misanthropic over the disappointing shallowness of the world, even of some of his friends, is bored by everyone. His statement, "So long as I have you I can never be unhappy . . . ," is a direct paraphrase of the author's famous pronouncement, couched in almost identical terms in the memoirs.[43]

Similarly, the narrator feels, "never should we be two strangers," a feeling strongly recorded all through the memoirs with regard to Simone de Beauvoir's attachment to Sartre. What is written in this story about André and his wife also goes for the author who had forsworn marriage. There are more such remarks, which, fitting the context of the story, at the same time recall the fundamental agreement between the two lifelong companions. Thus a passage where André snaps out of his morose and grouchy attitude, lucidly analyzing the self-pity that went into his childish conduct, is reminiscent of both the memoirs and, very strongly so, of the first novel, *She Came to Stay*, where Pierre had such moments of candor. At the same time, the passage alluded to in "L'Age de Discrétion" ("The Age of Discretion") is not without similarities to Sartre's story "La Chambre" ("Intimacy and other Stories").

If there is any philosophical point of view in the narration, it
would be the haunting awareness of the passage of time, which the
author was to develop more thoroughly in *La Femme Rompue (The
Woman Destroyed)*. In some ways, "The Age of Discretion" serves
as a tryout, an overture to *The Woman Destroyed*, less obsessive,
yet already self-centered and self-righteous in the point of view of
the narrator.

VIII *"Monologue" (1967)*

With its complete change of style, pace, content, this frantic so-
liloquy is a veritable tour de force. In this story, Simone de Beauvoir
uses the vulgar, spiteful jargon of a woman obsessed by her many
failures. Obliquely, we learn that she was first married to one of her
mother's old paramours; that the daughter born from that marriage
committed suicide at seventeen; that Murielle, the monologuizing
victim of society, gave up her happy liaison with Florent to marry
Tristan, a banker, now forty-five, who now lives separated from her.
She was given the apartment and a pension, provided Francis, their
son, stay with his father. Murielle rants against her upstairs
neighbors, who noisily celebrate Christmas; against the street full of
traffic and joyful hornblowing; against her mother, her brother—in
short, against everything and everybody. Her misanthropic, censorious mind is constantly at the breaking point, while she raves on
and on, firing her own sometimes lagging spirits with crude swear-
words. Moreover, everybody is dirty, everywhere she suspects sexual depravation and aggression against her sanity: thus, she feels,
people are conspiring to deprive her of her sleep. No matter that
silence follows the gleeful Christmas racket—her ambivalent fear
wants to "stop the uproar, the silence. . . . "[44] Such universal fear
and hatred, continuously denounced by her, show her impotence.
No one can be reached by her, and that very impotence feeds her
rancor. Hence the monologue.

The story is told in confused, elliptic, allusive spurts. The
monologuist is proud that she has always been frank to the point of
antagonizing people. When the little Murielle was asked: "And so
we love our little brother, do we?" she answered calmly: "I hate
him"—a scene which is repeated almost verbatim to serve as a sort
of leitmotiv.[45] "Monologue," too, serves as a harbinger for *The
Woman Destroyed*. Although constantly kept at fever pitch, the

narrative in its intensity foreshadows some of the heartbreak of the last portion of the triptych.

Christmas night is notoriously unpropitious for lonely people; it is a time when suicides are frequent. In her often scatological frenzy, few moments of lucidity occur, such as the musing: "I was made for another planet altogether; I mistook the way. . . . "[46] A final attempt to bring back Tristan to her apartment ends with Murielle threatening, over the phone, to commit suicide in the presence of their son, Francis. The whole story, breathless but not necessarily breathtaking, marks a departure from Beauvoir's naturally relaxed style and clear thinking. It is intentionally pathetic, showing the depth of misery found in loneliness and abandonment. But occasionally, by its very virulence, the tone falls flat. To sustain such an infernal mood throughout a story of this length (thirty-five printed pages) takes a certain virtuosity. The point of the monologue is driven home forcefully, perhaps too vigorously for artistic balance. The theme of the story is clearly that universal rancor produces more solitude.

Since we see the characters only through the incurably jaundiced eyes of the narrator, these characters fail to come to life; they remain shadowy: the extreme animosity of the monologuist can suggest only a fleeting silhouette. In its vignette form, this story fits in well enough with its companion pieces, all written around a single theme of loneliness, the passage of time, and betrayal by those once loved.

IX   La Femme Rompue (The Woman Destroyed, *1967*)

Simone de Beauvoir's next novel, a long lament on the passage of time and the frailty of human attachments, is both poignant and, at the same time, trying to read. Critics were divided, at the time of its publication, between those admiring the depth of psychological observation and those annoyed by the egocentricity of the narrator's viewpoint. Indeed, the narrator composes a fascinating paean to jealousy. Maurice, a physician doing scientific research, and Monique, his wife of twenty-odd years, have lived together in what appeared to her as a life of mutual love. All of a sudden, she is confronted with her husband's admission that he has a love affair with another woman, Noëllie Guérard, a successful lawyer, a divorcee with a thirteen year old daughter.

At first, Maurice tries to minimize the impact of this relationship on his marriage. When Monique, hurt in her feelings for her husband as much as in her pride, berates him for lying to her about the length of time he spends with Noëllie, he argues he lied only to spare her the suffering of knowing. Increasingly, by her very refusal to accept the situation, Monique contributes to alienating Maurice, who spends more and more time away from home. Her friends advise Monique not to antagonize Maurice so that she may appear magnanimous. She tries, but to no avail. Despite her good intentions, she cannot help provoking scenes that Maurice resents, though he professes to regret what in reality is the result of his infatuation with Noëllie. Monique can think of nothing but her predicament. All her friends urge her to be active, to take a job; she cannot stop brooding. Periodically, she will vent her jealousy over some new arrangement which creates an even greater distance between her and her husband, causing Maurice to attempt a half-hearted concession to his wife, that subsequently he will resent having made. At the end, it is clear that for all her desperate struggle against inevitable loss, Monique will live alone, having lost her self-respect as well as her husband's residual love.

Throughout the tense diary entries, we see a woman who, through an analysis of the past, tries to understand what went wrong and when. She anxiously asks her friends, and even her own daughters, at what point in her marriage the trouble began. Naturally, no one can answer her on that score, the disaffection having occurred slowly over the years without her realizing it. The account of Monique's suffering ought to be moving. Indeed, her pathetic loneliness shows real depth of perception on the part of the author. *The Woman Destroyed* has succeeded in recording the pangs of doubt, of gnawing uncertainty, the feeling of betrayal and of loss. It has done so more faithfully than any other book in this century, except perhaps for Proust's searching probe into jealousy. But in Proust, such feelings of anxiety, while keen and genuine, remain refined and distilled through urbanity. Here, raw passion replaces urbane restraint, and wild flights of vengeful dreams flare up only to smolder on unfulfilled.

On the debit side, it should be noted that the very intensity of Monique's constant suffering makes any objectivity in her account of events impossible. Maurice remains a one-dimensional figure, never shown in his own right, only in his reactions to his wife's queries. The same is true of the women characters; thus, the daughters are sketchily drawn. This may be all right for the domesticated Colette but leaves important questions unanswered in the case of the emancipated Lucienne, who would certainly have emerged less negatively had her mother been less distraught. What we learn about Lucienne suggests a complex character; as seen through Monique's eyes, she never becomes anything but a faceless, bloodless, lifeless skeleton. Thus, her episodic emergence at the very end of the novel is less than felicitous.

Despite these reservations, it must be said that *The Woman Destroyed* is an important literary document, a document already pointing the way to the author's ever-growing interest in women's rights and her commitment to the struggle for women's liberation. Technically, the novel is another tour de force, renewing the age-old device of the diarist or the writer of confession type fiction. True, Simone de Beauvoir is no second Benjamin Constant; her characters are intriguingly but nonchalantly strung around the pure line of Racinian passion. As they are all shown invariably through Monique's biased eyes and ears, such teichoscopical devices backfire more often than not, causing figures such as Diana, Isabelle, Marie, to be pale, indistinguishable foils to the vigorously drawn heroine. As for Noëllie, the immediate cause for Maurice's breach of faith, his wavering and instability, her role has adequate relief: nothing more need be known of her or about her than is suggested by Monique's strident fantasies and Maurice's reticence.

Monique needs no excuse in her bitter indictment of men, of all those who, she suspects, conspire to deny her her rightful happiness. Excuses are not needed, as the reader becomes sufficiently aware of the monomaniacal nature of Monique's obsession. Whereas in the past she had shown real interest in people and compassion for their misfortunes, now her own increasing misery, as she suffers from the effects of jealousy and gossip, closes her off from others. She had assumed a certain responsibility in persuading the wayward Marguerite to return, temporarily, to the center for delinquent girls, where stagnation and idleness drove these potentially good and sound girls to distraction. Now she completely abandons Marguerite to a fate of certain corruption and degradation. More and more self-centered, she relates every event to herself only; it takes monstrous egotism, after a long separation from her daughter in New York, to talk only about her own problem.

Monique contemplates suicide, but decides against it, more out of spite than for any positive reason. She allows herself to flounder in a state of stupor, dirt, neglect, and passivity during Maurice's absence on a skiing trip with Noëllie. The situation described in that episode is strongly reminiscent of *Thérèse Desqueyroux* by Mauriac, where for absolutely different reasons, a woman wallowed in self-pity and unhappiness. Monique records: "Nothing touches me anymore."[47]

The diary form has both great advantages—vigor, immediacy of perception—and some disadvantages: it is conducive to one-sided portrayal, and it ends up by omitting what might contradict the narrator's views. In spite of the appearance of painstaking sincerity—objectivity is impossible—in *La Femme Rompue (The Woman Destroyed)* there are some attempts at lay psychoanalytical exploration of the past, especially as regards the marriage. However, these, as well as the way in which Monique besieges her friends with questions, are intended to reestablish an impossible status quo. Thus all these consultations prove futile; Monique does not want advice, but is crying out for help. Hers is an heroic struggle against an injustice for which there is no remedy.

Far from representing all women in their fight for liberation and self-assertion, Beauvoir's heroine is depicted as an unhappy victim of society who might forego general justice for the sake of personal happiness. The underlying theme is male callousness, although Maurice is shown as a man without evil intent. A fictional male is not—not yet—the adversary.

On balance, Simone de Beauvoir's fiction commands respect, even if some of her novels were less appreciated than others. Her output in this field is honorable, though it may be safely asserted that her memoirs afford far more excitement to readers than most anything she invented. When her novels, or at least most of them, are forgotten, chances are that the memoirs will attract as many people as they do now.

CHAPTER 6

Conclusion

A NY evaluation of living writers is bound to be corrected and revised eventually. What will a retrospective analysis of Simone de Beauvoir's work reveal? No doubt, some of her writings will have lost the fascination they held for generations of contemporaries. Some of her works, however, are clearly destined to endure and foster interest in the foreseeable future. It may be an idle question to ask—as some critics have done—whether the novelist is more significant than the essayist or the memorialist. In my opinion, it is the close interrelationship between these three genres practiced by Simone de Beauvoir that makes her an important thinker of our time.

The novelist tackled difficult existential questions in fiction based in part on her own experience. The essayist addressed herself to the major problems of our time as well as to past ideas and the personal touch which Simone de Beauvoir applied to her writing humanized both these problems and ideas by concrete reference to life. The memorialist, through the remarkably candid presentation of her own life, synthesized burning issues of this century and the meaning of life altogether.

Most of the vilification of her work takes aim at her lifelong association with Sartre. That she is an autonomous thinker, a free and equal spirit, is easily seen from all her pronouncements when on her own. The intimacy with Sartre proved mutually beneficial and enriched both their lives and works. It takes extreme pettiness to refuse Simone de Beauvoir acknowledgment as a full-fledged intellectual and a fine and often original writer that she so amply deserves.

The vivaciousness and keen observation of Madame de Sévigné, perhaps without the marquise's lightness of touch; the ability to evoke passion, as found in Madame de Lafayette, without however her tact and her discretion; the superior grasp of matters intellectual and political of Madame de Staël, without her capriciousness and fondness for domination; the daring and also the deep social commitment of George Sand—and much, much more—these are some of the traits and talents that Simone de Beauvoir combines in her life and work, so closely interwoven.

Where others compromised or maneuvered, Simone de Beauvoir is blunt. She proves firm and principled in most instances where a point of conscience arises. That very outspokenness at times hampers the translator. In this context I must give praise to most of her translators, who, on the whole, did an admirable job rendering into fluent, often elegant English her frequently dense prose. The very intensity of her thought created ambiguities (e.g., in *The Coming of Age*) that have been eliminated in the translations. The result, curiously, is that while Beauvoir's expression is original, forceful, direct, the readers of the English version of her thought seldom if ever lose any of that directness and rather gain from the clarification of her expression, filtered into clear English more often than not.

The consistent seriousness of the writer is what seems to have caused irritation in many of her critics. Besides the generally nonchalant use of documentation, it is mostly the unswerving determination of the social innovator that upset some. Others reproached her for precisely the most sincere and genuine efforts at understanding this world. Appreciation is a matter of individual taste; but snap judgments are frequent among Beauvoir's most severe critics. To say, as Brigid Brophy once did, that "Sagan is the most underestimated and Mlle. de Beauvoir the most overestimated presence in postwar writing"[1] shows a view of French letters shared by few today.

It is probable that posterity will come to a more balanced judgment of Simone de Beauvoir's work. One recent investigation of the philosophic merit of her writings aptly and graphically demonstrates that she used literature to express philosophic ideas,[2] as previously noted in this study. Literature had overshadowed the early preoccupation with the explanation of the meaning of life. When I asked Madame de Beauvoir why she had not written more literary essays—in view of the incisiveness of her acumen as shown in her views on Sade—she answered: "Things did not happen that way; I would have liked to do more in that vein. . . . "[3] There was no need for her to regret such omission, since the totality of her work to date represents a rich harvest.

Too much has been made of the famous phrase the memorialist, with her characteristic candor, recorded in which Sartre, early in their relationship, had called her "a clock inside a refrigerator": her personal warmth, her loyalty to her friends prove the contrary. While she now fends off would-be intruders on her privacy and her time, once she agrees to see people she is by no means intimidating or arrogant. Her superior mind needs no superficial satisfaction, and the way she sought the understanding of young people, not only during the 1968 student upheaval but consistently over the years, shows an intelligent, responsible person bent on the problems of her time, particularly problems of the young and the workers, who always find a sympathetic ear in her and women's problems, which now take precedence over many others—but that does not mean that she closes her mind to many other very real problems. Her study of ageing is only the latest in a sequel of earnest endeavors at contributing to progress.

Just as in the Alps the wanderer discovers first one high peak, then another even higher behind the first one, and climbing on sees more towering summits emerge, so the work of certain writers appears like a mountainous mass where the tops of the individual mountains seem higher, from the distance, one than the other. This image, of course, has been used in didactic illustrations of literature textbooks to emphasize the relative importance of different works by classical writers, so I may be forgiven, I trust, for using an old cliché to illustrate the situation of a contemporary writer's work. To tell which of Simone de Beauvoir's books is the most important is a matter of distance and balanced appreciation. *She Came to Stay, The Second Sex, The Mandarins, A Very Easy Death,* the memoirs, and *The Coming of Age*—all are books of remarkable impact in our time. Just which is the most significant is hard to tell. Taken in its entirety, the work of Simone de Beauvoir proves meaningful to her contemporaries the world over. The writer grew to become a public figure, respected by many, reviled by some. The test of time alone can establish her place in French letters. Already, women's liberation movements in the whole world acclaim her as a pioneer, a leader, and she now more or less reluctantly accepts this role.

I would say, on balance, that Beauvoir's assets by far outweigh her faults. If her style is often sloppy, her notions of research casual, nevertheless her message is clear. Her vision at all times remains impressively dominant, never domineering. One of the major figures in twentieth century thought, she easily outshines the mass of writers. Ageing sensibly and gracefully, living to the fullest her enormous potential with open eyes and a clear, unimpaired mind, she remains one of the few forces for the good in our world.

Notes and References

Preface

1. A French novelist whose work received the Grand Prize of the Académie Française, and whose most famous novel was discussed by Simone de Beauvoir in the first volume of her memoirs, changed his mind completely: where she had been a degenerate misfit—and worse—in his opinion before he had read a single line by her, she became a respectable author when, for reasons of self-esteem, he started reading her.

Chapter One

1. *Memoirs of a Dutiful Daughter*, translated by James Kirkup (Cleveland and New York, 1959), p. 34. Henceforth all references to this work will be incorporated into the text.

2. Bernard le Bovier de Fontenelle (1657–1757), as quoted in *The Age of Enlightenment*, edited by Otis Fellows and Norman Torrey (New York, 1942), p. 60; also in *Oeuvres choisies de Fontenelle* (Paris, n.d.).

3. Joseph von Eichendorff (1788–1857), *Aus dem Leben eines Taugenichts (Life of a Good-for-Nothing)*; also in the poem, put to music by Mendelssohn, "Der Frohe Wandersmann" (second stanza): "Die Trägen, die zu Hause liegen, Erquicket nicht das Morgenrot. . . ."

4. *The Prime of Life*, translated by Peter Green (Cleveland and New York, 1962), p. 178. Henceforth all references to this work will be incorporated into the text.

Chapter Two

1. It is amusing to note that the translator of the first volume of memoirs committed a rather substantial boner of his own: the author, speaking of Sartre and his friends, faced with military service, writes: "Ils se moquaient de l'ordre bourgeois; *ils avaient refusé de passer l'examen d'E.O.R.*" The italicized portion means that they had refused to take the equivalent of the ROTC examination. The translation reads: "they had refused to sit for the examination in religious knowledge."

2. "Le fignolage ne fut jamais fort."

3. *Mémoires d'une jeune fille rangée* (Paris, 1958), p. 364: "je ne faisais pas le poids."

4. It is necessary to read what causes that feeling of impotence: "Chamson poussait des cris de triomphe: 'Qu'est-ce qu'on leur met!'—'Chamson ne met rien du tout, à personne,' dit Sartre avec impatience. Palabrer, déclamer, manifester, prêcher: quelle vaine agitation! Nous aurait-elle paru aussi dérisoire si l'occasion nous avait été donnée de nous y mêler?"

Chapter Three

1. *Force of Circumstance*, translated by Richard Howard (New York, 1964), p. vi. Henceforth all references to this work will be incorporated into the text.

2. *Tout compte fait* (Paris, 1972), p. 134.

3. *A Very Easy Death*, translated by Patrick O'Brian (New York, 1966), p. 12. Henceforth all references to this work will be incorporated into the text.

4. Elizabeth Janeway, *New York Times Book Review*, September 4, 1966, p. 5.

5. Pierre-Henri Simon, *Le Monde*, November 12–18, 1964.

6. Ibid.

7. *All Said and Done*, translated by Patrick O'Brian (New York, 1974), Prologue, p. ii. Henceforth all references to this work will be incorporated into the text.

8. *Tout compte fait*, p. 37: "on écrit à partir de ce qu'on s'est fait être, mais c'est toujours un acte neuf."

9. A list of all the major boners committed by Simone de Beauvoir throughout her work would have to be furnished here; such a list is easy to compile from reviews and other critiques.

10. *Tout compte fait*, p. 159: "Je suis quelque peu bibliophage . . . "; "The Last Testament of an Intellectual," *Times Literary Supplement*, May 24, 1974, p. 543.

Chapter Four

1. Pierre Brunel et al., *Histoire de la Littérature Française* (Paris, 1972), p. 672.

2. *Pyrrhus et Cinéas* (Paris, 1944), p. 90; also in *La Longue Marche* (Paris, 1957).

3. Jean-Paul Sartre, *L'Etre et le Néant* (Paris, 1943), p. 561.

4. Henri Peyre, *French Novelists of Today* (New York, 1967), p. 250.

5. Jean Bruneau, "Existentialism and the American Novel," *Yale French Studies*, I (1948), 70.

6. Henri Peyre, "Existentialism—A Literature of Despair?" *Yale French Studies*, I (1948), 24.

7. Germaine Brée, "Existentialism," in *Dictionary of French Literature*, edited by Sidney D. Braun (New York, 1958), p. 116.

8. Henri Peyre, *French Novelists of Today*, p. 245.

9. Ibid., p. 249.

10. Ibid., p. 250.

11. *L'Existentialisme et la Sagesse des Nations* (Paris, 1948), p. 9. Henceforth all references to this work will be incorporated into the text.

12. *La Force des Choses* (Paris, 1963), p. 80.

13. *The Second Sex*, translated by H. M. Parshley (New York, 1968), p. xxiii. Henceforth all references to this work will be incorporated into the text.

14. Liliane Sichler, "Simone de Beauvoir au pays de la vieillesse," *L'Express*, June 26, 1978, pp. 62–63.

15. Robert D. Cottrell, *Simone de Beauvoir* (New York, 1975), p. 94.

16. *The Coming of Age*, translated by Patrick O'Brian (New York, 1972), pp. 8–9. Henceforth all references to this work will be incorporated into the text.

17. These are the last words of the book, before the Appendixes. "Changer la vie" is also the title of a volume of reminiscences by Jean Guéhenno. If the reference is deliberate, that is a piquant novelty, as Sartre held Guéhenno in less than high esteem: in *Nausea* he is mocking him.

Chapter Five

1. Cf. Brian Fitch, *Le Sentiment d'Etrangeté chez Malraux, Sartre, Camus et Simone de Beauvoir* (Paris, 1964), p. 149: "combien la part de l'imagination est mince dans la création romanesque. . . . "

2. John Cruickshank, ed., *The Novelist as Philosopher*, Studies in French Fiction 1935–1960 (London, 1962).

3. Chapter Four of the present study contains a short outline of existentialism.

4. The debate on this novel went indeed beyond literary criticism and spilled over into the public domain.

5. *L'Invitée*. (Edition du Livre de Poche–Gallimard 1964), p. 268: "est-ce qu'ils savaient que tout était faux? Ils savaient sûrement."

6. Ibid., p. 419: "elle . . . lui demandait . . . seulement de la laisser participer à sa vie . . . "

7. Xavière's act obviously derives from Nietzsche, who, in school, let a lighted match burn out on his palm.

8. *The Prime of Life*, p. 270; also quoted by Fitch, p. 150.

9. Fitch, p. 162: "Si le rapport de Françoise et de Pierre est peu satisfaisant, il nous faut reconnaître la réussite de l'auteur, par contre, dans sa description du dévoilement de la conscience de Xavière." Another model for Pierre was the actor Dullin.

10. Gaëtan Picon, *Panorama de la Nouvelle Littérature Française*, 22nd edition (Paris, 1951), p. 97.

11. *Le Sang des autres* (Paris, 1945), p. 173.

12. Cf. Serge Julienne-Caffié, *Simone de Beauvoir* (Paris, 1966), p. 160.

13. *Le Sang des autres*, pp. 38–40.

14. Ibid., p. 96: "la malédiction d'être un autre."

15. Ibid., p. 146: "Gauthier was a pacifist. Paul was a communist. Hélène was in love. Laurent was a worker. And I was nothing at all."

16. Ibid.

17. *La Force de L'Age*, p. 599.

18. Maurice Nadeau, *Le Roman Français depuis la Guerre* (Paris, 1963), p. 114.

19. Ibid., pp. 115–16.

20. Picon, p. 97.

21. *The Prime of Life*, p. 465.

22. Ibid.

23. Julienne-Caffié, pp. 162–63.

24. Frances Keene, "Deathless Hero," *New York Times Book Review*, January 20, 1955.

25. Maurice Cranston, "Simone de Beauvoir," in *The Novelist as Philosopher*, p. 161.

26. *Les Mandarins* (Paris, 1954): "Paule le regarda . . . : 'on ne rompt pas avec un ami de vingt-cinq ans . . .' " (p. 379); and "Quinze ans d'amitié effacés en une heure" (p. 401). *The Mandarins*, translated by Leonard M. Friedman (Cleveland and New York, 1960): "Paula looked at him . . . : 'You don't break up a friendship of twenty-five years' standing . . .' " (p. 404); and "Fifteen years of friendship wiped out in a single hour" (p. 427).

27. Cf. the Louise Perron episode in *The Prime of Life* (pp. 136–45); the surname is obviously the one the author chose for Henri, in *The Mandarins*—another illustration of irony.

28. *The Mandarins*, p. 592.

29. Ibid., p. 55.

30. Ibid., p. 45.

31. "Devant la souffrance d'un enfant, *La Nausée* ne fait pas le poids." *Le Nouvel Observatur* Sept. (?) 1964(?)

32. *The Mandarins*, p. 76; also restated in *The Prime of Life*, p. 396.

33. Jean-Paul Sartre, "La République du Silence," in *Situations*, III, 11.

34. A few voices out of the broad spectrum of critics should suffice. From the sensible appraisal by Pierre de Boisdeffre, *Une Histoire vivante de la Littérature Française d'Aujourd'hui* (Paris, 1958), p. 111, who finds *The Mandarins* "lewd" ("impudique") but has praise for the dialogue; through the timid indignation of Hourdin, p. 141, who finds the "erotic scenes quite unnecessary" to the lenient view of a Dominican priest, A. M. Henry, whose book, *Simone de Beauvoir ou l'Echec d'une Chrétienté* (Paris, 1961) is

concerned only marginally with the writer; he focuses his interest on her education, her intellectual and moral formation. The upshot, in the present context, is that certain movies of the "nouvelle vague" are far more to blame than Beauvoir's writings—if blame one must. Finally, at the lowest possible level, written under the pen name La Vouldie, *Madame Simone de Beauvoir et ses Mandarins* contains very little substance and is mostly innuendo and imputation of motives.

35. *Les Belles Images*, translated by Patrick O'Brian (New York, 1968), pp. 127–28.

36. Marc Slonim, "European Notebook," *New York Times Book Review*, Jan. 15, 1967.

37. Etienne Lalou, "La Raison n'a pas toujours Raison," *L'Express*, December 12–18, 1968, pp. 43–44.

38. Charles Poore, book review in the *New York Times*, March 6, 1968.

39. Lalou.

40. *The Woman Destroyed*, translated by Patrick O'Brian (New York, 1969), p. 21. "The Age of Discretion" is the first story in the book.

41. Ibid.

42. Ibid., p. 22.

43. Ibid., p. 34. "Je savais qu'aucun malheur ne me viendrait jamais par lui à moins qu'il ne mourût avant moi." *La Force de L'Age*, p. 28. ("I knew that nothing bad would ever happen to me on his account unless he were to die before me.")

44. "Monologue," in Ibid., p. 89.

45. Ibid., pp. 91, 104.

46. Ibid., p. 110.

47. Ibid., p. 216. (On the book as a whole, Evan S. Connell, Jr., writes in the *New York Times Book Review*, February 23, 1969, p. 4. "Two long stories and a short novel on the menace of middle age. The only unsatisfactory thing about them is that they are not fiction. . . .")

Chapter Six

1. Brigid Brophy, *New York Times Book Review*, May 9, 1965, p. 1.

2. Chantal Moubachir, *Simone de Beauvoir ou le souci de différence* (Paris, 1972.)

3. Interview the author had with Simone de Beauvoir, April 7, 1974.

Selected Bibliography

PRIMARY SOURCES
(First editions only indicated, fiction marked with an asterisk)

*L'Invitée. Paris: Gallimard, 1943.

She came to stay. Cleveland and New York: World Publishing Company, 1954.

Pyrrhus et Cinéas (essay). Collection Les Essais, #15. Paris: Gallimard, 1944.

*Le Sang des autres. Paris: Gallimard, 1945.

The Blood of Others. Translated by Roger Senhouse and Yvonne Moyse. New York: Alfred A. Knopf, 1948.

Les Bouches inutiles (play). Paris: Gallimard, 1945.

*Tous les Hommes sont mortels. Paris: Gallimard, 1946.

All Men are mortal. Translated by Leonard M. Friedman. Cleveland and New York: World Publishing Company, 1955.

Pour une Morale de l'Ambiguïté (essay). Paris: Gallimard, 1947.

The Ethics of Ambiguity. Translated by Bernard Frechtman. New York: Philosophical Library, 1948.

L'Amérique au jour le jour. Paris: Morihien, 1948.

America Day by Day. Translated by Patrick Dudley. New York: Grove Press, 1953.

L'Existentialisme et la Sagesse des Nations (essays). Paris: Nagel, 1948.

Le Deuxième Sexe (essay). 2 vols. Paris: Gallimard, 1948.

The Second Sex. Translated by H. M. Parshley. New York: Alfred A. Knopf, 1953.

*Les Mandarins. Paris: Gallimard, 1954.

The Mandarins. Translated by Leonard M. Friedman. Cleveland and New York: World Publishing Company, 1960.

Privilèges (essays). Collection Les Essais, #76. Paris: Gallimard, 1955. Partial translation: "Must we burn de Sade?" Translated by Annette Michelson. London: Weidenfeld & Nicholson, 1953.

La longue Marche. Essai sur la Chine. Paris: Gallimard, 1957.

The Long March. Translated by Austryn Wainhouse. Cleveland and New York: World Publishing Company, 1958.

Mémoires d'une jeune fille rangée. Paris: Gallimard, 1958.

Memoirs of a Dutiful Daughter. Translated by James Kirkup. Cleveland and New York: World Publishing Company, 1959.

Brigitte Bardot and the Lolita Syndrome. London: Deutsch, Weidenfeld and Nicholson, 1960.

La Force de l'Age. Paris: Gallimard, 1960.

The Prime of Life. Translated by Peter Green. Cleveland and New York: World Publishing Company, 1962.

Djamila Boupacha. In collaboration with Gisèle Halimi. Paris: Gallimard, 1962.

Djamila Boupacha. Translated by Peter Green. New York: MacMillan, 1962.

La Force des Choses. Paris: Gallimard, 1963.

Force of Circumstances. Translated by Richard Howard. New York: Putnam, 1964.

Une Mort très douce. Paris: Gallimard, 1964.

A Very Easy Death. Translated by Patrick O'Brian. New York: Putnam, 1966.

*Les Belles Images. Paris: Gallimard, 1966.

Les Belles Images. Translated by Patrick O'Brian. New York: Putnam, 1968.

*La Femme rompue. Paris: Gallimard, 1967.

The Woman Destroyed. Translated by Patrick O'Brian. London: Collins, 1968.

La Vieillesse (essay). Paris: Gallimard, 1970.

The Coming of Age. Translated by Patrick O'Brian. New York: Putnam, 1972.

Tout compte fait. Paris: Gallimard, 1972.

All Said and Done. Translated by Patrick O'Brian. New York: Putnam, 1974.

SECONDARY SOURCES

BRÉE, GERMAINE, *Women Writers in France:* Variations on a Theme. New Brunswick, Rutgers University Press, 1973. From the Middle Ages to our day, a finely comprehensive overview and analysis with a substantial discussion of Beauvoir's writings.

CAYRON, CLAIRE. *La Nature chez Simone de Beauvoir.* Collection Les Essais, #185. Paris: Gallimard, 1973. A subtle, sensitive, congenial analysis, going far beyond the announced scope; very good bibliography.

COTTRELL, ROBERT D. *Simone de Beauvoir.* New York: Frederick Ungar, 1975. A concise, competent critical monograph.

CURTIS, ANTHONY. *New developments in the French Theatre.* London: Curtain Press, 1948. Close analysis of *Les Bouches inutiles.*

DESCUBES, MADELEINE. *Connaître Simone de Beauvoir.* Collection Connaissance du Présent. Paris: Editions Resma, 1974. Useful for the research of themes.

FITCH, BRIAN T. *Le Sentiment d'Etrangeté chez Malraux, Sartre, Camus et Simone de Beauvoir.* Les Lettres Modernes. Paris: Minard, 1964. The chapter on Simone de Beauvoir is one of the best explanations of ideas, images, characters in modern literature; the whole volume is brilliant.

GAGNEBIN, LAURENT. *Simone de Beauvoir ou le Refus de l'Indifférence.* Preface by Simone de Beauvoir. Paris: Editions Fischbacher, 1968. Fair and judicious study of the work and the stature of the writer.

GENNARI, GENEVIÈVE. *Simone de Beauvoir.* Collection Classiques du XXe siècle. Paris: Editions Universitaires, 1958. Brief, independent view of the early work.

HENRY, A. M. o.p. *Simone de Beauvoir ou l'Echec d'une Chrétienté.* Collection Le Signe. Paris: Arthème Fayard, 1961. This book, by a Dominican priest, is concerned only marginally with Simone de Beauvoir as a writer or even as a person. Her education, her intellectual and moral formation, the "failure" of various parochial schools, and the writer's Catholic parents are the object of this study, which strives to be fair to the writer's work.

HOURDIN, GEORGES. *Simone de Beauvoir et la Liberté.* Collection Tout le Monde en parle. Paris: Editions du Cerf, 1962. Uneven but somewhat valuable attempt by a Christian critic at evaluating Simone de Beauvoir's thought.

JEANSON, FRANCIS. *Simone de Beauvoir ou l'Entreprise de vivre* (suivi de deux entretiens avec Simone de Beauvoir). Paris: Editions du Seuil, 1966. A comprehensive, fine-grained, and most enlightening explanation of the work. Jeanson's undisguised partiality is innovative and does not prevent him from being soundly critical.

JULIENNE-CAFFIÉ, SERGE. *Simone de Beauvoir.* Collection Bibliothèque Idéale. Paris: Gallimard, 1966. Factual presentation with synopses of works and sample pages; has fairly good bibliography.

LASOCKI, ANNE-MARIE. *Simone de Beauvoir ou l'Entreprise d'écrire.* The Hague: Martinus Nijhoff, 1971. A careful, comprehensive explication with valuable bibliography, including Italian, Spanish, and above all Polish studies on the writer.

LA VOULDIE (pseudonym). *Madame Simone de Beauvoir et ses "Mandarins."* Collection Libres Paroles. Paris: La Librairie Française, 1955. A curiously virulent pamphlet, accusing the novelist of being a "Jacobin"; vilification of the Liberation; the author holds that *The Mandarins* is a call for assassination.

LEIGHTON, JEAN. *Simone de Beauvoir on Woman.* Foreword by Henri Peyre. London: Associated University Presses, 1975. Primarily based on the literary works, this is a precise yet delicate and luminous interpretation of feminism in the works of Simone de Beauvoir.

LILAR, SUZANNE. *Le Malentendu du Deuxième Sexe.* Paris: Presses Universitaires de France, 1969. As polemics go, this is a spirited reply to Simone de Beauvoir's thesis.

MADSEN, AXEL. *Hearts and Minds.* The Common Journey of Simone de Beauvoir and Jean-Paul Sartre. New York: William Morrow and Company, 1977. Attractive and entertaining, this quite well-documented book describes most of the lives of the two authors; some of the points made will raise some eyebrows, especially in the synopses of books and plays, but also with regard to the presentation of ideas.

MARKS, ELAINE. *Simone de Beauvoir: Encounters with Death.* New Brunswick: Rutgers University Press, 1973. Far and away the best monograph on Simone de Beauvoir. A superior demonstration of themes essential to any understanding of the work.

MOUBACHIR, CHANTAL. *Simone de Beauvoir ou le souci de différence.* Collection Philosophes de tous les Temps. Paris: Seghers, 1972. Highly competent and felicitously clear definition of ideas and trends.

NAHAS, HÉLÈNE. *La Femme dans la Littérature existentielle.* Paris: Presses Universitaires de France, 1957. Gives a wealth of details and some useful indications.

RECK, RIMA DRELL. *Literature and Responsibility.* The French Novelist in the 20th Century. Baton Rouge: Louisiana State University Press, 1969. On Beauvoir—as well as on the other subjects of analysis—a lucid and painstaking study of literary and psychological themes.

SCHMALENBERG, ERICH. *Das Todesverständnis bei Simone de Beauvoir.* Berlin: de Gruyter, 1972. A theological investigation, leading to new insights, valid for literature, too.

VAN DER BERGHE, Christian Louis. *Dictionnaire des Idées: Simone de Beauvoir.* Collection Dictionnaire des Idées. The Hague: Mouton, 1967. A useful compendium.

WASMUND, DAGNY. *Der Skandal der Simone de Beauvoir.* Probleme der Selbstverwirklichung im Existentialismus, dargelegt an den Romangestalten Simone de Beauvoirs. Münchner Romanistische Arbeiten. Munich: M. Hueber, 1963. A thoughtful, ingenious interpretation of the concept of "scandal." Among the many doctoral dissertations seen, by far the best. Self-realization in existential thought as illustrated by Beauvoir's characters turns out to be a key to many other revelations.

Index

195